By John Paterson

THE PRAISES OF ISRAEL

THE GOODLY FELLOWSHIP OF
THE PROPHETS

Charles Scribner's Sons

THE
PRAISES OF ISRAEL

THE PRAISES
OF ISRAEL

*Studies Literary and
Religious in the Psalms*

by

JOHN PATERSON

Professor of Hebrew and Old Testament
Exegesis, Drew Theological Seminary,
Madison, N. J.

NEW YORK
CHARLES SCRIBNER'S SONS
1950

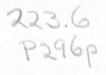

To

the Memory

of

John Edgar McFadyen

FOREWORD

The Psalmist seems to be the forgotten man of the Old Testament. Volumes innumerable have been written concerning the voice of God to his people as it came by the mouth of the prophets or lawgivers. Considerably less attention has been directed to the other side of this matter, the cry of man to God for deliverance from the down-drag of his lower self, or his yearning prayer, amid the darker problems of human existence, for light upon his path, or, yet again, the ringing cry of joy with which he greets the wondrous deliverances of his God. The writer has long felt the need of a good book on the Psalms though he does not presume to think he has supplied that need. But what is written here was written first for his own needs and it is offered to those who, as teachers or preachers, are called upon to unveil the mystery of God, and to that wider public who feel that not all the things of time and sense can satisfy the heart in which God has set eternity.

The main purpose of this volume is to show the enduring vitality of *the Praises of Israel*. Thus the author has sought to show how the Psalter grew like a living thing and how from the beginning it was closely entwined with the life of the worshiping community. The Psalms spring from life and speak to life. In this connection he has sought to convey to the general reader the results of recent critical research which have issued in a fresh approach to, and fuller understanding of, these Hebrew songs, which constitute a veritable Golden Treasury. The second section consists of a short series of expository studies to illustrate the main types of song in the Psalter. The third section is doctrinal in character and seeks to set forth the deep spiritual insights of the Psalms in regard to God, Man, Nature, Sin, Grace, and the Life Hereafter.

In the citation of the songs the Authorised Version has been used on the ground that this may be the form most familiar to the reader. Frequently, where a more exact sense was required, the translation has been made direct from the Hebrew. Use has also been made of the *Metrical Version* (Oxford Press) in the belief that many will be interested to see the form in which these ancient songs are still sung in modern public worship. This version of the Psalms is "authorised for use in public worship" in the Presbyterian churches of Scotland, Ireland, Canada, Australia, New Zealand, and South Africa. A number of these metrical versions of the Psalms is included in many of our American hymnaries.

The author desires to express his indebtedness to Dr. Julius A. Bewer, Professor-emeritus of Hebrew in Union Theological Seminary, New York; and to the late Dr. James Moffatt, of the same Seminary. To their wise counsel and suggestion he owes much. Thanks are due also to Mrs. F. Heisse Johnson who prepared the indices.

The author would like to think that what he has written may help others to a better understanding and fuller appreciation of *the Praises of Israel*.

JOHN PATERSON

Drew Theological Seminary
Madison, N. J.

CONTENTS

ix

PART III   The Religious Teaching of the Psalter

THE
PRAISES OF ISRAEL

1

THE PRAISES OF ISRAEL

The Psalter has been called the hymnbook of the second temple (537–37 B.C.), but that title is misleading and conveys little as to its real value and permanent significance. The Psalter has become the hymnbook of the Church Universal, the peculiar possession of all God's children. That is the more wonderful inasmuch as the songs of yesteryear pass quickly into the discard and are covered with oblivion. But the *Praises of Israel* never grow old. Age does not wither them nor custom stale their infinite variety. "In it," says W. T. Davison, speaking of the Psalter, "beats the very heart of the Old Testament and of all spiritual religion." [1] Here we have a veritable "bunch of everlastings." They possess the secret of eternal youth. Age after age turns to this refreshing fountain for comfort and renewal and finds here "a well of water springing up to everlasting life." Here we are "brought to the banqueting house, and his banner over us is love, and his fruit is sweet to our taste." Man does not live by bread alone and here the soul of man, be he Jew or Gentile, through all the centuries has learned to go out and to come in and find large sustenance. Here we find in fuller

[1] *The Praises of Israel,* p. 1.

3

measure than elsewhere those vital realities "by which men
live and wholly therein is the life of the spirit." "Deep call-
eth unto deep." The Psalter finds us in the deepest parts of
our being, and those songs speak a universal language to the
heart of all mankind.

We scarcely realise what is involved here. The thing is
passing strange. This people with whom those songs originated was the Jewish people. Theirs was a small land, smaller
than the state of Vermont: they were wholly insignificant
in the commerce and traffic of the East. Moreover, they had
a spirit of national pride and exclusiveness such as was found
nowhere else. Concerning them Tacitus, the Roman his-
torian, says: "The Jews are extremely loyal toward one another, and always ready to show compassion, but toward
every other people they feel only hate and enmity." [2] The
Jews were unpopular in antiquity and the passage of time
has not diminished that unpopularity. Nonetheless the songs
they sang have become the welcomed possession of all mankind. The 100th Psalm may have been sung first in the
temple at Jerusalem, but it has become the "gathering song"
of God's people everywhere. Its lofty strains are heard on
"India's coral strand" and by "Afric's sunny fountain,"
while, too, it is heard on the rolling pampas of the South
and the wide plains of the West and beneath the Southern
Cross:

> All people that on earth do dwell
> Sing to the Lord with cheerful voice:
> Him serve with mirth His praise forth tell,
> Come ye before Him and rejoice.[3]

These *Praises of Israel* have become the spiritual treasure
of all the world: this is the hymnbook of Everyman. The
Psalms belong to all believers. Whether the worshiper's Zion

[2] Tacitus, *Histories*, V, 5.
[3] In this section the psalms are cited from *the Psalter in Metre, authorized for use in Public Worship*, Oxford Univ. Press.

be a noble cathedral or a humble edifice in the lonely places, where may he find fuller expression of his love for the sanctuary and the "place where God's honour dwells" than in the words of Psalm 84?

> How lovely is thy dwelling-place,
> O Lord of hosts to me!
> The tabernacles of thy grace,
> How pleasant, Lord, they be!

When Luther seeks a song to relieve adequately his heart that bursts to praise he finds it in the 46th Psalm:

> God is our refuge and our strength,
> in straits a present aid:
> Therefore although the earth remove
> we will not be afraid.

And so *Ein feste Burg ist unser Gott* becomes the marching song of the Protestant Reformation and the 46th Psalm greets the larger dawn of spiritual freedom. Could anything more profound be said by the penitent soul than the words of Psalm 130? Here is a minor melody for the sad soul that is oppressed by the weight of sin:

> Lord, from the depths to thee I cry'd,
> my voice, Lord, do thou hear:
> Unto my supplication's voice
> give an attentive ear.

> Lord, who shall stand, if thou, O Lord,
> shouldst mark iniquity?
> But yet with thee forgiveness is,
> that feared thou mayest be.

Or could anything be more comforting to the heart that longs for the peace and joy of forgiveness than to hear those words that soothe the troubled spirit?

> Praise waits for thee in Zion, Lord,
> to thee vows paid shall be.
> O thou that hearer art of prayer,
> all flesh shall come to thee.

Iniquities, I must confess,
   prevail against me do:
But as for our transgressions, Lord,
   them purge away shalt thou.

(PSALM 65:1–3)

Or will the redeemed ever find more fitting words to express
their boundless joy for what God has done than those used
by the singer in Psalm 103?

O thou, my soul, bless God the Lord,
   and all that in me is
Be stirred up his holy name
   to magnify and bless.
Bless, O my soul, the Lord thy God,
   and not forgetful be
Of all his gracious benefits
   he hath bestowed on thee.

We are not yet too far removed from V-E Day and V-J Day
to remember the feeling of release and emancipation that
came to us with the end of hostilities. It fell to the present
writer to conduct the service of thanksgiving for victory on
V-J Day and how he regretted it was impossible to have
sung the triumph song of Israel! There is nothing to equal
it in any of our modern hymnals.

Now Israel
   may say, and that truly,
If that the Lord
   had not our cause maintain'd
If that the Lord
   had not our right sustain'd
When cruel men
   against us furiously
Rose up in wrath
   to make of us their prey;
Then certainly
   they had devour'd us all,
And swallow'd quick,
   for ought that we could deem;
Such was their rage,
   as we might well esteem.

And as fierce floods
   before them all things drown,
So had they brought
   our soul to death quite down.
The raging streams,
   with their proud swelling waves,
Had then our soul
   o'erwhelmed in the deep.
But bless'd be God
   Who doth us safely keep,
And hath not giv'n
   us for a living prey
Unto their teeth
   and bloody cruelty.
Ev'n as a bird
   out of the fowler's snare
Escapes away,
   so is our soul set free;
Broke are their nets,
   and thus escapèd we.
Therefore our help
   is in the Lord's great name,
Who heav'n and earth
   by his great pow'r did frame.

                               (PSALM 124)

It must appear as a sheer wonder of the spirit that songs composed and conceived in such a narrow atmosphere should possess such elements of universality and that they can be fitted into every time and clime and find such large welcome. Yet so it is.

"More than any other book of the Old Testament," says Davison, "it has been baptized into Christ." [4] Today we bind the Psalter with our New Testament and thus show by physical proximity its fundamental spiritual affinity. Nor is this a modern discovery. From earliest times the Christian church has treasured the Psalter: of 287 quotations from the Old Testament appearing in the New, 116 are taken

---

[4] *Op. cit.,* p. 2.

from the Psalter. This was the hymnbook of the early church: the hymn which our Lord and his disciples sang on that last night ere "they went out to the mount of Olives" (Matthew 26:30) was the *Hallel,* Psalms 113–118. Paul and Silas in the prison at Philippi (Acts 16:25) forgot the pain of their beaten bodies as they sang those old Hebrew songs. Plain practical James counseled his hearers:

> Is any among you afflicted? Let him pray.
> Is any merry? Let him sing psalms.
>
> (JAMES 5:13)

That the Psalms were in common use in the church at Corinth is clear from I Cor. 14:26. When Christian hymns were first introduced they were based on the Psalms as models. The *Gloria in Excelsis* is a kind of Christian *Hallelujah,* while the *Magnificat* of Mary (Luke 1:46–55) and the *Benedictus* of Zachariah (Luke 1:66–79) are both in form and content echoes of the Psalter. The Psalter was

> the first book which the early church put into the hands of her young converts, the primer of her religious teaching: and no man could be admitted to the highest order of the clergy unless he knew the Psalter by heart. It was used for singing in the first assemblies for Christian worship, and it has ever continued to be used, sometimes as the sole book of praise, and always as the best and most enduring of all.[5]

Church hymnaries may come and go but the Psalter goes on for ever.

No other book appears to have entered so deeply into the general life of humanity. It has made a permanent impress on all ranks and classes of men. The noble families of England are proud to have its words inscribed upon their coats-of-arms, the Beauchamps with the motto: *Fortuna mea in bello campo* (Psalm 16:6: *The lines are fallen to me in*

---

[5] Robertson, James, *Poetry and Religion of the Psalter,* pp. 7, 8.

pleasant places), the Coghills with: *Non dormit qui custodit* (Psalm 121:3: *He that keepeth thee shall not slumber*), and the Comptons with: *Nisi Dominus frustra* (Psalm 127:1: *Except the Lord do build the house they labor in vain that build it*), which last is also the motto of the capital city of Edinburgh. Ancient universities, such as Oxford, find here the legend of their charter: *Dominus illuminatio mea* (Psalm 27:1: *The Lord is my light*). Great business corporations, such as the Butchers' Company, turned to the Psalter for their mottoes, and, appropriately enough, the Butchers found their most suitable legend here: *Omnia subjecisti sub pedibus, oves et boves* (Psalm 8:6, 7: *Thou has put all things under his feet, sheep and oxen*). Sundials, coins, rings, trenchers, and even sword blades have all been engraven with texts from the Psalms. No portion of life seems to remain untouched by the grace and beauty of this volume. It has spoken to the heart of humanity through all the ages. It is a mirror of life.

If further proof of this last statement is required let the reader turn to the volumes of Rowland E. Prothero (Lord Ernle) [6]—to whom we are indebted for some of the foregoing illustrations—and John Ker,[7] wherein is recorded the abiding influence of the Psalter on life and history through all the ages. We will content ourselves here with one reference. It will be to John Wesley. The incidents connected with his conversion are known to the world. He has told us [8] that:

> In the evening I went very unwillingly to a society in Aldersgate Street, where one was reading Luther's preface to the Epistle to the Romans. About a quarter before nine, while he was describing the change which God works in the heart through faith in Christ, I felt my heart strangely warmed.

[6] *The Psalms in Human Life.*
[7] *The Psalms in History & Biography.*
[8] *Journal*, Vol. 1, pp. 101–102 (Everyman edition).

But in the preceding paragraph of the *Journal* he tells us what preceded that Aldersgate experience:

> In the afternoon I was asked to go to St. Paul's. The anthem was "Out of the deep have I called unto thee, O Lord; Lord, hear my voice. O let thine ears consider well the voice of my complaint. If thou, Lord, will be extreme to mark what is done amiss, O Lord, who may abide it? But there is mercy with thee; therefore thou shalt be feared. O Israel, trust in the Lord: for with the Lord there is mercy, and with him is plenteous redemption. And he shall redeem Israel from all his sins."

And so the experience of the *De Profundis Clamavi* led to that strange heart-warming at Aldersgate and the *Gloria in Excelsis* as with proper Pauline emphasis he records: "I felt I did trust in Christ, Christ alone, for salvation; and an assurance was given me, that he had taken away *my* sins, even *mine,* and saved *me* from the law of sin and death."

The Psalter is worthy of our study. If any doubt lingers as to its value, let us hear the words of the great Reformers. Let Luther first appear to testify:

> Where are more beautiful words of joy than the Psalms of praise and prayer? There thou seest into the hearts of all the saints, as into fair and pleasant gardens, as into heaven itself, and walkest amongst the heart-rejoicing flowers, the happy and gladsome thoughts which rise to God and his goodness. And again, where findest thou deeper and more touching words of sorrow than in the Penitential Psalms? There thou seest again into the heart of all the saints, as if into death or hell itself. How dark and gloomy it is there when God hides his face! And when they speak in fear and hope, it is in such words that no painter could give the colors and no Cicero the language.[9]

And Calvin will here be one with Luther:

[9] Preface to the Revised Edition of the German Psalter, 1531.

I may truly call this book an anatomy of all the parts of the soul, for no one can feel a movement of the Spirit which is not reflected in this mirror. All the sorrows, troubles, fears, doubts, hopes, pains, perplexities, stormy outbreaks by which the hearts of men are tossed, have been here depicted to the very life.[10]

[10] Preface to Commentary on the Psalms, 1563.

2

THE GROWTH OF THE PSALTER

We speak here of the growth rather than compilation of the Psalter, for compilation seems too mechanical a term to designate what we have here. We shall see later that the Psalter was closely bound up with the life of the worshiping community and, as we have already seen in the introduction, the book is characterized by such a sheer vitality that we must attribute to it a life of its own. It is something that has grown by its own inherent power, and, if we must think of a compiler, we will think of one who has brought together vital utterances that had in themselves the capacity to endure. Like a mighty spreading oak it has grown through the centuries: the book as we now have it is the outgrowth of the piety and devotion of countless generations.

i

The Psalter, as it lies before us in our Bibles, is divided into five books, each of which is clearly marked off by a closing doxology. Thus we have the first book (1–41) in which most of the psalms bear the inscription "a Psalm of David," and the book closes with the doxology:

Blessed *be* the Lord God of Israel from
everlasting, and to everlasting. Amen and Amen.

Psalms 72:18, 19; 89:52; 106:48 form the closing doxologies
of the second, third, and fourth books respectively, while
Psalm 150 is itself an expanded doxology and fitly closes the
last book. These divisions may be original in some cases, but,
inasmuch as the third and fourth books contain precisely
the same number of psalms and the division between Psalm
106 and 107 seems arbitrary and inappropriate, there is reason to believe that this division into five books is the artificial device of an editor. It may well be that, as "the five
fifths of the Law (Genesis–Deuteronomy)" represented the
voice of God to the congregation of Israel, so the "five fifths
of the Psalter" represented the answering voice of the congregation to God. We may pass by this artificial form of the
Psalter and examine the book itself to see what evidence it
affords of gradual growth and development. Such an examination will reveal that it grew from less to more and that
the Psalter is composed of several little Psalters and that
various minor collections were in circulation before the book
assumed its final form.

Quite clearly we are dealing with a long process that lasted
through many centuries. W. F. Albright "would date the
contents of the Psalter in their present form between the
eleventh and fourth centuries B.C., and would admit a date
many centuries higher for the Canaanite substratum of
many psalms." [1] This is certainly not the view of the Psalter
that has been held generally, but it is nearer the truth, as
the present writer sees it, than the position of Pfeiffer [2]
(whom Albright is criticising in the foregoing quotation),
Duhm, [3] and other scholars who would relegate the majority

---

[1] *Journal of Biblical Literature,* Vol. LXI, Part 2, p. 122.
[2] Pfeiffer, R. H., *Introduction to the O. T.,* pp. 619f.
[3] Duhm, Bernhard, *Die Psalmen.*

of the psalms to the Maccabean period. It has been customary to refer to the Psalter as the hymnbook of the second
temple and to proceed on the assumption that when the
first temple was destroyed (586 B.C.) all the spiritual treasures of Israel were lost. Such an assumption is wholly unjus-
tified. Israel took her spiritual treasures to Babylon, and
among these treasures was her treasury of song (Psalm 137).
The military might of Babylon might destroy the body politic, but it could not kill the national soul or rob them of their
spiritual heritage. Those treasures went to Babylon with the
exiles and they returned in an enriched and enhanced form.
It was good for Israel that she was afflicted. The second
temple was not something completely *de novo*, as J. M. P.
Smith [4] seems to suggest: it inherited the traditions of the
first temple and was built on its foundations. There is an
amazing continuity in the history of Israel such as is not
found in the history of the great empires that oppressed
and enslaved her. That continuity is there because Israel's
might was not revealed in material things but in the realm
of spirit.

ii

Israel's history opens with song (Exodus 15:20) and the
Psalter does not contain all the Hebrew songs. These are
found all through the Old Testament, and just as there were
many collections of the English ballads or the folk songs of
Europe, so there were many collections of Hebrew songs.
These collections originate at different periods and in different places, and older songs may have persisted and found
place in later collections. In the continuing process such
older songs would be modified and brought down to date to
suit the taste and circumstances of later periods. Old hymns
are continually being modernised until many of the original

---

[4] *The Psalms,* p. 247.

features are lost in the process. One can observe that from a study of the Wesley hymns, and that the same thing happened with the Hebrew songs there seems no reason to doubt. Psalm 14 with its parallel in Psalm 53 or II Samuel with its parallel in Psalm 18 reveals the process in operation. That our Psalter may contain songs by David is not to be denied: the persistent witness of the Old Testament in this matter cannot be disregarded (Amos 6:5; II Samuel 1:17; 3:33). But it may be doubted whether songs originating in such a rude period would remain through the centuries without undergoing considerable modification. They had to be adapted and modernised for a later and more sophisticated period. The lyric that first springs from individual experience must later be fitted to the use of a worshiping congregation, and a universal hymnbook will necessarily shed all features of the local and individual. This is not intended to deny the presence of Davidic psalms in the Psalter but only to indicate how such songs were liable to modification in the course of time. Psalmody is older far than David's time and the parallels from Egypt, Babylon, and Ugarit show that psalmody had reached a high state of development before the establishment of the monarchy in Israel.

We may leave this question aside and proceed to consider the separate collections that make up our book of Psalms. That separate collections did exist is evident from one or two striking facts. In the first place we have "doublets" in the Psalter, the same psalm appearing twice. It does not seem at all likely that if one writer composed or compiled the book he would have inserted the same song twice. Yet this is what we find. Psalm 14 reappears as Psalm 53 and Psalm 40:14–18 is repeated as Psalm 70, while Psalm 31:3 is duplicated by Psalm 71:1–3. Psalm 58:8–12 together with Psalm 60:7–14 constitute Psalm 108. These were evidently popular songs that found place in more than one collection. This can be explained satisfactorily only by the fact that an editor or compiler has put together different collections.

In the second place there is a striking difference between the group 1–41 and the group 42–83 in the use of the Hebrew term for deity. Psalm 14, for example, is repeated in Psalm 53 but in the earlier Psalm the writer uses the name of Israel's covenant God, Jehovah or *Yahwe,* while in Psalm 53, the writer uses the more general term for deity, *Elohim* (God). This variation in the use of the terms for deity provides a clue as to the origin of the first two books of the Psalter. In the first book Jehovah (*Yahwe*) is used regularly while from 42–83 the word *Elohim* (God) is employed to the almost total exclusion of the other term. In Psalms 1–41 the word Jehovah is used 272 times while *Elohim* occurs only 15 times. In the group 42–83 *Elohim* occurs 200 times and Jehovah 42 times. Obviously the writer or editor of this second group of songs was anxious to remove the sacred name (YHWH, *Yahwe*) from the text and substitute a more common term. In Psalm 50:7 we read: "I am God (*Elohim*) thy God" which is a quotation from Exodus 22:2 where we read: "I am Jehovah (*Yahwe*) thy God." Similarly in Psalm 45:7 we read: "God, thy God, hath anointed thee," where it is clear that an original *Yahwe* has been replaced by a later *Elohim,* the original reading being: "Jehovah, thy God hath anointed thee" (*Cp.* also Psalm 43:4; 82:1). The reason for this editorial process is not exactly clear, but it would seem to be due to a theological interest. In post-exilic Judaism the name *Yahwe* or Jehovah was regarded as ineffable, too sacred to be spoken. Various substitutes were employed in its stead, of which the most common is *Adonay.* Though the word Jehovah appears in our texts it is never spoken or pronounced by the Jews. In the Hebrew text (which had no vowels originally) the word YHWH

(*Yahwe*) was supplied with the vowels of *Adonay* and is
so read in the Jewish service. It was the failure of the King
James translators to understand this practice that led to the
hybrid form *Jehovah*: this term contains the consonants
(JHVH) of the ineffable name and the vowels of its substitute *Adonay*. The form Jehovah is impossible in Hebrew,
but it is too deeply embedded in popular usage to be
changed. The Greek Bible translated the term in most instances by *Kyrios* (Lord), and in this it was followed by the
Authorised Version. The American Standard version renders
regularly by Jehovah.

iii

Thus far we have evidence of two main collections, 1–41
and 42–83, the former being often called the Jehovistic and
the latter group the Elohistic Psalter from their respective
use of the terms Jehovah or Elohim for deity. Within the
first group we note that all but four of the songs bear the
title: "a Psalm of David." Psalms 1 and 2 may have been
regarded as introductory and are without title: Psalm 10 is
really part of Psalm 9 and in the Greek is one with it. Psalm
33 is the only real "orphan" in the collection, though in the
Greek it is ascribed to David. Thus the first book may be
called *Davidic*.

In the second group we can discern various lesser groups.
Psalm 50 together with Psalms 73–83 constitute a group of
twelve songs attributed to the professional singing guild, the
Sons of Asaph. Psalms 42–49 represent another smaller
group assigned to another guild, the Sons of Korah. With
respect to these professional guilds of temple singers it
would seem that the Sons of Asaph enjoyed a higher pres-
tige than their colleagues, the Sons of Korah. It would appear that the latter had been promoted from the position of
doorkeepers in the temple and had attained the higher dig-

nity of serving in the ministry of music and song. Difficult questions of history are involved here and we need not enter into the question. Both Gunkel [5] and Kittel [6] are of opinion that the Sons of Korah attained the higher dignity about 300 B.C.

In addition to these minor groups we find here another group of songs ascribed to David. At the end of Psalm 72—ascribed to Solomon—we read the words: "the prayers of David, the son of Jesse, are ended." This must mark off a collection of "David" psalms between 51–72, all of which, with three exceptions (66, 67, 71), are ascribed to David, for after Psalm 72 we find another eighteen songs of David in Books 3–5. Here, then, we have a second "David" collection which has been edited by an Elohistic redactor. Moreover, an appendix has been added to this Elohistic Psalter and in Psalms 84–89 we have four more psalms from the guild of Korah (84, 85, 87, 88), one ascribed to David (86) and another to Ethan the Ezrachite (89). That this forms an appendix to the Elohistic Psalter (42–83) is obvious from the fact that it has not been subjected to the editorial revision which Psalms 42–83 have undergone. The word Jehovah is used freely and no attempt has been made to change it.

Thus we can see the various steps in the growth and development of the Psalter. We have here

a) The first "David" collection with closing doxology (1–41)
b) The second "David" collection with closing doxology (51–72)
c) Two Levitical guild collections (42–49; 50, 73–83).
d) Elohistic redaction and combination of b) and c)
e) Addition to d) of non-Elohistic supplement with doxology (84–89)
f) Formation of the collection 90–150

[5] Gunkel-Begrich, *Einleitung in die Psalmen,* p. 442.
[6] Kittel, Rudolph, *Die Psalmen,* p. xxi.

With reference to f) there is not much to be said. Barnes calls it "the anonymous collection," for most of the songs in this group lack a title or superscription. Seventeen are ascribed to David, one to Moses (90), one to Solomon (127), but the majority are without name. Nevertheless, certain smaller collections are found here, of which the most compact group is that consisting of fifteen songs, generally called "Songs of Ascents" or "Psalms of Degrees" (120–134). They are sometimes called the "Pilgrim Psalms."

Another group within this large collection consists of the "Hallel" psalms (113–118), known as the "Hallel of Egypt" and sung at the Passover service. Psalm 136 is known as "the Great Hallel," while another group of the same type extends from Psalm 146–150. Psalms 105–107 constitute a trio of "Hōdū" (Give thanks) songs, each of which opens with the word *Hōdū:* these are similar to the Hallel songs. Whether these formed little separate groups or not cannot be determined with certainty. The other songs seem to be largely anonymous productions assembled by the editor: we may call the whole group "the anonymous collection."

iv

We may pause here to consider the meaning of the term "David" in the expression *a Psalm of David*. The phrase need not suggest authorship though it has been usually interpreted in that sense. The Hebrew expression *le-David* could equally well be translated "to David" or even "after the style of David." The same form is applied to the songs of the guild singers: *a psalm to (or of) Aspah, a psalm to (or of) the Sons of Korah*. Quite clearly these titles cannot signify authorship, for songs are not written by groups or guilds but by individuals. It may be that *of David* here denotes a collection of songs in the style and manner of David, and the collection was known as "David's." Thus the phrase would simply denote a particular collection to which the song belonged.

The superscriptions which have been set over the songs show clearly that *of David* was interpreted as signifying authorship. These superscriptions frequently purport to give the precise events in the life of Israel's king that moved him to utter the song. But the superscriptions are demonstrably unhistorical and they are devoid of value for the interpreter. The Hebrew Bible sets *of David* before seventy-three psalms; the Greek Bible adds fifteen more. The Greek Bible ascribes Psalm 137 to David but the contents of the psalm show it was written in Babylon. Psalm 139 is ascribed to David but it is simply inconceivable that the king who conceived of Jehovah as a localised deity in I Samuel 26:19 could speak such terms of universalism in Psalm 139. Moreover, the Hebrew language of Psalm 139 is a debased form of Hebrew, while in David's day the language was in its classical form, as may be seen from a study of the Court Journal in II Samuel 9-20. The ideas expressed in this psalm are among the loftiest in the Old Testament, but such ideas were not present in David's time. Just as all Law was ascribed to Moses and all Wisdom to Solomon so men tended in that early time to assign all songs to David.

As to the order in which these various collections were brought together it is not possible to speak with certainty. The first book (1-41) is generally regarded as earliest in time. Speaking generally the psalms of most archaic cast (18, 19a, 24b, 29) are found in this group. Nevertheless Pfeiffer [7] would date Psalm 2 about 103 B.C. and Psalm 33 seems to be a late insertion. Though little store is to be set by these superscriptions it is significant that Psalm 90 is ascribed to Moses and Psalm 127 to Solomon. The Elohistic group is later than Book 1, and the appendix to that group

[7] Pfeiffer, R. H., *op. cit.*, p. 628.

(84–89) must be later still. In the last group (90–150) we seem to have a more intimate connection with the religious cult and public worship: this would accord with the developments in the period of the second temple. Eissfeldt [8] would accept the dates suggested earlier by Steuernagel and assigns Book 1 to the fifth century B.C. when the professional guilds seem to have played no prominent part, while the group 42–83 he would assign to the fourth century when such guilds were in their heyday. Psalms 90–150 he would assign to the third and second centuries B.C. when the greater guilds had lost their prominence through an increase in their number (I Chron. 25:8–31). Further than that we may not go with assurance save to say that the final compilation of the Psalter marks the end of a process which had continued through many centuries.

From all we know of the history of the Old Testament Canon it would appear that the Psalter attained its present form, or a form almost identical with it, by the beginning of the second century B.C. It was translated into Greek about 150 B.C. and Psalm 79 is quoted as Scripture in I Maccabees 7:16. I Maccabees may be dated as early as 125 B.C. There is no reason to think that the Greek version, as originally translated, contained less than our Psalter and was supplemented later to bring it into accord with the Hebrew. Furthermore, we have a group of eighteen psalms entitled "the Psalms of Solomon," translated into English by Ryle and James under the revealing title "Psalms of the Pharisees." These can be dated about 50 B.C. They differ in style and contents from our Psalter to such a degree that most scholars would set an interval of at least one hundred years between them and the Psalter.

This dating of the Psalter does not accord with the position of Duhm and many others who find the origin of most

[8] Eissfeldt, Otto, *Einleitung in das A. T.*, p. 502.

of the psalms in the Maccabean age. The present writer finds himself in agreement with Gunkel [9] and Oesterley [10] who hold that the presumed historical references and background of the Psalter are capable of interpretation from earlier periods of Hebrew history.

[9] Gunkel, Hermann, *Die Psalmen.*
[10] Oesterley, W. O. E., *The Psalms* (2 vols.).

3

A FRESH APPROACH TO THE PSALTER

The Psalter is worthy of study and in recent years much study has been devoted to it. Modern scholarship has shed a great deal of light here and it is now possible to make a fresh approach to the book. For the Psalter is a difficult book to interpret, and that for various reasons. In the first place there is the general character of Hebrew speech which is different from anything we are accustomed to.

> The Northern speeches imitate the sounds of Nature, but they do this roughly, and, as it were, only from without. They creak, rustle, hiss, and jar like the objects themselves ... but the further south we go the more delicate becomes the imitation of Nature. The words have passed through the firmer medium of emotion, and are framed, as it were, in the heart. They yield us, therefore, not coarse reproductions of sound, but images on which feeling has impressed its softer seal, thus modifying them from within.[1]

We in these northern latitudes are used to speaking with the

[1] Herder, J. G., *Geist der hebräischen Poesie*, Vol. II, pp. 13f.

teeth: we sound our vocables against our dental equipment and force the sound outward. But southern Europeans, *e.g.* the Italian people, do not speak so but rather with the *ore rotundo* and have a much fuller utterance and more animation in expression. But when we pass to the Orient and the eastern Mediterranean we find a speech that is not from the teeth nor with the *ore rotundo*: it is a speech deep-set in the chest with all the force of the abdominal and visceral muscles behind it. It is a speech with all the lifeblood of the heart behind it, and it is full of passion. It is removed *toto caelo* from Greek moderation or Latin deliberation. The Hebrew speech is characterised by extraordinary vitality and forcefulness and it abounds in deep gutturals which we can hardly frame to express. This must be borne in mind as we read those ancient songs.

Again the Hebrew does not think as we do. His thought processes differ from ours. His mind is intuitive in its working: it is not philosophical. He does not co-ordinate and relate things into a system as does the Greek. The pearls here all lie loose and unstrung: ideas are discrete and separate. The Hebrew doth not normally think logically. Jesus is not Socrates. Nor is there in Hebrew a system of particles, as in Greek or German, to indicate shades of meaning and stages of transition in the thought. The Hebrew thinks with the eye: the connection is optical rather than logical. He sees one thing, then another, and frequently the connection between these things may not be obvious to us. For example, how can we understand such a Psalm as the 23rd unless we think with the eye? Most commentators stumble here: they think the song lacks unity. It begins with a pastoral scene and suddenly at the fifth verse the scene seems to change to an indoor banquet:

> Thou preparest a table before me in the presence
> of mine enemies:

thou anointest my head with oil;
my cup runneth over.

(PSALM 23:5)

But surely the scene is still pastoral. The poet sees the sheep
and the shepherd and he sees the little black tent in the
desert, the shepherd's house of hair. He sees, too, the fugitive from blood revenge fleeing across that desert and behind
him are the avengers of blood. But if that fugitive can reach
that tent or even only touch the ropes of it he is safe, safe
as the rock of Gibraltar. For such is the law of hospitality
in the desert. That shepherd will take all he has and set it
before the fugitive: he will anoint the fugitive's head with
oil and give his best provisions as a banquet while the
avengers must stand without. There is nothing they can do
but wait. For this hospitality has a limit—two days and the
intervening night. For that period he is safe, but after that
period he must arise and go forth and bear his bloody assize.
As the poet looks on this and thinks of the hospitality of
God which is without limit he says:

Surely goodness and mercy shall follow me all the
days of my life;
and I will dwell in the house of the Lord for ever.

(PSALM 23:6)

When we think thus with the eye, the unity of the pastoral
scene is seen to be maintained from beginning to end. That
is to think with the eye.

Again it should be borne in mind that these songs were
sung and that the singer accompanied his songs with lively
gestures. Behind these songs is the Oriental singer with all
his Oriental idiosyncrasies. At times we can follow his *apode-
ictic* gestures, as in Psalm 36:12, where the words, "There—
there are the wicked fallen" are accompanied by a pointing
finger. At times we may miss the gesture and our interpretation will go astray. This principle, indeed, can be given a

much wider reference that yields significant results. May we not think that many of our Lord's words would gain fuller meaning and added significance if we thought of them as uttered with a smile or even with a merry twinkle in his eye? The Psalmist has given us a picture of *le Dieu qui rit* (the laughing God) in Psalm 2:4, and the Gospels not infrequently indicate that the Savior showed various emotions and made various gestures on different occasions. Did He not smile as He said to the Syro-Phoenician woman,

> It is not meet to take the children's bread
> and to cast *it* to dogs.

And did He not smile again at her quick rejoinder,

> Truth, Lord; yet the dogs eat of the crumbs
> which fall from their master's table.
>
> (MATTHEW 15:26, 27)

It is difficult not to think so, and, if we could only think that way, it might often save us from turning poetry into prose, and it would vitalise our appreciation of the Word. The reporter gets the words but it is the camera that gets the pictures. Truth is mediated by personality.

Furthermore, we are all so dull and pedestrian in our modes of thought and behavior that we forget the Oriental was quite otherwise. He loves hyperbole, and exaggeration is his normal mode of speech. All his geese are swans. He draws the long bow. Nor need we seek to impose upon him our Procrustean molds of thought or try to rule his exuberant fancy. Imagination will take flight and soar into the empyrean where we cannot or will not follow. But we must not seek to clip his wings with the "abhorred shears" of our own matter-of-factness. Much in the Psalter would become clear to us if we kept in mind this Oriental characteristic. When the Hebrew sings of his king no epithet is too lofty for use: he will call him "God's son" (Psalm 2:7), and even "God" (45:6), though this latter flight has seemed too dar-

ing to many commentators who seek to evade it or explain
it away. The court poet in his exuberance could say of
Solomon:

> His name shall endure for ever:
> His name shall be continued as long as the sun:
> And men shall be blessed in him:
> All nations shall call him blessed.
>
> (PSALM 72:7)

Language like that might be suitable in world empires such
as those of Egypt or Babylon, and such language is used of
these monarchs. But the Hebrew could think lofty thoughts
about his own little kingdom: its poets did not fail to dream
dreams and see visions.

> He shall have dominion also from sea to sea,
> And from the river unto the ends of the earth.
>
> (PSALM 72:8)

Solomon was certainly the subject of great expectations, but
then the Hebrew knew that there was a great God behind
and above Solomon. His land might be small but his God
was a great God above all gods.

There is yet another difficulty in understanding the Psalter. It is the difficulty of interpreting the Hebrew tenses.
Hebrew had only two tenses for the verb, one referring to
action completed and the other to action incompleted.
These, however, are used in a somewhat confusing fashion,
and this confusion gives rise to varying interpretations. Like
the prophets who do not see God's action in front of them
(future), but as already accomplished and behind them
(past), and use the *prophetic perfect* or past tense to describe an action which God is about to do as already done,
so to the eye of these poets and their lively faith future pre-
dictions are frequently put in the past tense. Promises of
blessing yet to be realised are described as already fulfilled,
for with God to think and to do are one and the same thing.

God speaks and it is done. Reality to them is not what we see but what God sees, and this reality is present to the prophetic vision and to the psalmist's faith. Thus, for example, Psalm 46, which on the basis of the past tenses might be referred to some great historical deliverance—generally assumed to be that from Sennacherib in 701 B.C.—can equally well be referred to a future promise of salvation, and is so interpreted by Gunkel.

Considerations such as these will indicate the difficulties that beset the path of those who would have a full understanding of the Psalter. In recent years, however, striking progress has been made in the direction of a more adequate interpretation of the Psalter. For this progress we are indebted mainly to two Continental scholars, Hermann Gunkel[2] and Sigmund Mowinckel.[3] As a result of their researches we have now come by a better understanding and a fuller appreciation of the book. Hitherto, interpretation has tended to move on the line of historical reference and from earliest times students of Scripture have sought to find suitable occasions in the history of Israel which might have given rise to particular psalms. It is easy to understand how one might associate Psalm 46 with the deliverance from Sennacherib in 701 B.C. or Psalm 51 with David's repentance after his great sin. We have many superscriptions to the psalms and these may be considered man's earliest effort to provide an introduction to the Psalter. The necessity for such an introduction arises as soon as a generation emerges which is too far removed from the writing in question to understand it without some explanation of its origin. These superscriptions were not written by the original singers, but have been added by later editors who desired to elucidate

---

[2] Gunkel, *Die Psalmen* (*Göttinger Hankkommentar zum Alten Testament*, II, 2); Gunkel-Begrich, *Einleitung in die Psalmen.*

[3] Mowinckel, Sigmund, *Psalmenstudien* I–VI.

the song by stating its original occasion or background. Thus in Psalm 30 we have the superscription, "a psalm and song at the dedication of the house of David," but this is plainly unhistorical. The song is the song of an individual and later it was given this national interpretation. In Psalm 34 we read in the superscription, "a psalm of David when he changed his behavior before Abimelech who drove him away, and he departed." Here the later editor has forgotten his history and made a strange lapse, for Abimelech was contemporary with the patriarch Isaac: the king in question here is Achish of Gath (I Samuel 29). Editors can slip and this one did. Such assignments of historical occasions are quite arbitrary and fanciful: there is no support for them in the text of the Psalms. It may seem strange to us, but there is scarcely one historical reference in the Psalter. That need not surprise us if we bear in mind that a hymnbook designed for general use must be purged and cleared of all particular reference. The Psalms that are so personal in their appeal are devoid of personal references. "This poor man" of the Psalter, like the father of the Prodigal Son, is any man, Everyman.

It is precisely this fact that has constrained scholars, and particularly the two named in the foregoing, to seek a new approach to the Psalter. This new approach proceeds on the line that *these songs originate in the religious cult and are associated with the worship of the community.* The songs may, therefore, be classified and clarified by investigation of this reference.

4

CLASSIFICATION OF THE PSALMS

The interpretation of the Psalter, which we have designated "a fresh approach," begins with the idea that these songs were originally cult songs and were used in close relation with the worshiping community. Each type of song was associated with a particular occasion in the religious life of the community. When that occasion is determined, we have the *vital reference* or, as Gunkel calls it, the *Sitz im Leben*, of the song. Such is the living background of the psalms.

Furthermore, each literary type will be found to be characterised by a definite literary form with regular recurring formulae as well as by a clear and definite content. Obviously this approach is along the line of literary history, and it is the merit of Gunkel that he has proceeded on this definite line, and given us a series of literary Types or *Gattungen* as he names them. Thus he writes: "The basic fact for the literary study of the Psalms is that these songs spring originally from worship. These Psalms must be assigned to a class whose common element is some definite divine service." [1] Gressmann is one with Gunkel in this view when he

[1] *Old Testament Essays* (Society for O. T. Study), pp. 124–125.

says: "The religious festivals, the sacrifices and rites, the whole of the public and private sacrificial worship, are inconceivable if the sacred ceremonial was not accompanied by psalms. Word and ritual act cannot be separated in the sphere of religion any more than in that of magic." [2] Thus definite religious ideas and moods will help us to determine the type to which a particular psalm belongs. It is easy enough to distinguish between songs of sorrow and songs of joy, and classification of the psalms has been frequently made on the basis of their contents. But this criterion has proved inadequate and has led to confusion, and a more adequate criterion is necessary. Such a criterion can be found in the literary form and structure of the psalms. Gunkel classifies according to the *regular recurring formulae of each particular type*. Here we are dealing with something wholly objective and impersonal: Hebrew poetry is highly impersonal in the sense that its literary forms and molds are fixed and rigid. One can scarcely overemphasise this fact, for it is the failure to recognise this on the part of Mowinckel that has deprived his valuable studies of their highest value. Mowinckel has centered on the contents rather than on the literary form and has failed to observe Gunkel's caution as to the application of subjective criteria. The form is the thing in the literature of the Old Testament, and there is no such freedom and licence as is found in our own modern poets. The passionate thoughts of Job and Jeremiah were poured into molds which they did not create but inherited. These molds had a cast-iron rigidity which we fail to appreciate.

There seems no reason to question Gunkel's arguments or his exposition of them, and, while we agree with Löhr,[3] and with Gunkel himself, that this method of classification by

[2] *The Psalmists* (edited by D. C. Simpson), p. 11.
[3] Löhr, M., *Psalmenstudien* (BWAT, NF., Heft 3), p. 4.

form and structure may not be a key that will open every door, it is a method and approach that will take us further and yield more satisfying results than any previous method of interpretation. Gunkel holds that in this matter he is doing for the elucidation of the Psalter what Linnaeus did in the realm of botany.

i

Thus we may proceed to examine these classifications. On the ground of literary form and structure he finds the following main Types (*Gattungen*) which we set forth in order.

1. Hymns, or Songs of Praise. Subdivisions within this main group are the "Enthronement Psalms" and "Songs of Zion."
2. Laments of the Community.
3. Royal Psalms.
4. Laments of the Individual.
5. Thanksgiving of the Individual.

Most of the songs in the Psalter can be classified under these main groups, but there are smaller groups or Types, sometimes represented by only one or two psalms. Such are the following:

6. Blessings and Curses.
7. Pilgrim Psalms.
8. Thanksgiving of the Community.
9. Legends.
10. Psalms Dealing with the Law.
11. Prophetic Psalms.
12. Wisdom Psalms.

In addition there are psalms that may be classed as mixed types (*Mischgattungen*).

Such is Gunkel's classification in outline and we may consider the lines on which his scheme is constructed. In this connection we shall consider first the literary form of the Hymn.

Hymns from Babylon and Egypt are familiar enough and these possess a high degree of antiquity. Canaanite parallels, too, are present from Ugarit. But the hymn is found in early Hebrew literature, and the form or mold in which it is set is clearly defined from beginning to end. Miriam's song by the Sea of Reeds reveals the form:

> Sing ye to the Lord, for he hath triumphed gloriously;
> The horse and his rider he hath thrown into the sea.

> (EXODUS 15:21)

A psalm such as Psalm 117 will reveal the form in the Psalter:

> O praise the Lord, all ye nations;
> Praise him all ye people.
> For his merciful kindness is great toward us:
> And the truth of the Lord *endureth* for ever.
> Praise ye the Lord.

A greater prolixity may be found in the Magnificat (Luke 1:46f) or the Song of the Redeemed (Revelation 5:9) but the form has the same outline throughout. It consists of an introductory call to praise (*praise ye*) with reason annexed (*for*), followed by the main piece or *corpus,* and ending frequently with a renewed call to praise, as in the psalm just quoted. The invitation or summons to praise may vary according as it is addressed to choir or congregation, "Sing ye" or "Let us sing," or it may be put in the form of resolve, "I will sing." It might again take the form of a summons to one's own soul, "Bless the Lord, O my soul," or as in Psalm 8 it might vary the summons and adopt the form of an opening exclamation, "O Lord our lord, how excellent is thy name in all the earth": the same form recurs in Psalm 84. A further variation is seen in Psalm 18 where the transition from the introduction is made by a series of terms in opposition:

> I will love thee, O Lord, my strength,
> O Lord, my fortress and my deliverer,
> My God, my rock, in whom I take refuge;
> My shield, my horn of salvation, my lofty tower.

Yet again the transition may be effected by a simple relative clause:

> I will bless the Lord who hath given me council.
>
> (PSALM 16:7)

Or the form may be turned into the passive as in Psalm 124:6:

> Blessed be the Lord
> Who hath not given us *as* a prey to their teeth.

though this form is of rather rare occurrence in the Psalter.

More frequent is the use of the participle which is usually translated in our versions by the relative clause:

> Bless the Lord, O my soul,
> And all that is within me *bless* his holy name.
> Bless the Lord, O my soul,
> And forget not all his benefits:
> Who forgiveth all thine iniquities;
> Who healeth all thy diseases;
> Who redeemeth thy life from destruction;
> Who crowneth thee with lovingkindnesses and
>   tender mercies.
>
> (PSALM 103: 1–4)

Here the words "who forgiveth," "who healeth," "who redeemeth," "who crowneth" are represented in the Hebrew by the present participle of the verb. In some songs, for example, the Songs of Zion (Psalms 46, 48) the introduction seems to be omitted and the singer bursts right into song and into his main piece. Other hymns, like Psalm 150, seems to be no more than expanded introductions. Such variations gave vitality to the songs and saved them from monotony.

Those hymns were associated with the joyous occasions in the national life when the people assembled to the sanctuary to adore and praise their God for his grace and favor. This is the subject of their praise and, in the main piece or corpus of the hymn, they dwell adoringly on the goodness of God and sing of his mighty acts. Babylonian hymns usually begin in the same fashion, but they end with petition and one cannot escape the impression that the worshiper is flattering the deity with honorific epithets in order to secure his own personal ends. With the Hebrew the hymn is wholly theocentric and composed of pure praise. The hymn, too, may be sung antiphonally by two choirs or groups of worshipers, but the form is the same throughout. The hymn in its earliest stages may have been as much a cult act as the sacrifice itself: it was probably regarded as an offering that added strength to the deity. Such an idea may seem primitive and savoring of magic to our way of thinking, but early peoples did not think as we think.

While the hymn sings normally of God and his greatness, some of these hymns sing rather of the Holy City and extol the pride and beauty of Zion. The Hebrew could not refrain from extolling the place where God's honor dwelt. Such songs constitute a sub-group of the Hymn class and are classed as "Songs of Zion" (*Zionlieder*). In the Psalter are six such psalms (46, 48, 66, 84, 87, 122), and they are distinguished from the other hymns in that they sing of his glorious dwelling-place rather than of God himself. It may be observed here that Gunkel sometimes assigns a psalm to more than one class or group: Psalms 84 and 122 which he sets among the "Songs of Zion" are also classed as Pilgrim Psalms (the only real representatives of that group in the Psalter).

Attention must be called to another sub-group of the hymns. These are the "Enthronement Psalms," and around this group much discussion has centered. Mowinckel [4] and Volz [5] have contended strongly for the existence of an "Enthronement Festival" in early Israel, in which, amid the loud shouting of the people and the blowing of the ram's horn (*shōfar*), God ascends the throne on New Year's Day and proceeds to judge the world. Such a festival is known to us from Babylon, where on New Year's Day the god, represented by the king, ascends the throne in the course of a great ritual procession. A whole ritual-pattern is in question here, and many scholars [6] would infer that this pattern was originally presented in Hebrew worship. Mowinckel maintains that this was the main festival of the year and he ascribes a great many psalms to this group. Not only so, but he would deduce the origin of eschatology [7] from this ritual. But it has to be said that there is no direct reference anywhere in the Old Testament to any festival, although the ideas associated with the festival in Babylon are strongly present in the ritual of the Jewish New Year's Day. It would seem that Mowinckel, Volz, and Hans Schmidt have ventured further than the available evidence permits and have moved too far under the influence of a most seductive idea.[8]

As to the number of such psalms in our Psalter we are forced back upon the criterion of literary form. Mowinckel finds such psalms all through the book and tends to assign any psalm that speaks of a procession to this particular class. But, clearly, there must have been other festivals and other processions in Hebrew religious life. Gunkel, Eiss-

---

[4] Mowinckel, S., *Psalmenstudien II, Die Thronbesteigungsfest und der Ursprung der Eschatologie.*

[5] Volz, P., *Das Neujahrfest Jahwes (Laubhüttenfest).*

[6] *Myth & Ritual,* edited by S. H. Hooke.

[7] Mowinckel, S., *Psalmenstudien II.*

[8] This judgment is confirmed by N. H. Snaith in his recent volume, *The Jewish New Year Festival.*

feldt,[9] and Oesterley [10] would limit the number of such psalms to those songs that contain the recurring formula, "The Lord is (or is become) king." Such psalms are Psalms 47, 93, 96–99. Here we observe the value of Gunkel's literary criterion, and we see how vague things may become (as in the case of Mowinckel) when regard is paid only to ideas and content.

ii

Laments of the Community form a second main type. These are marked by a definite literary form and they are employed on particular occasions in the national worship. Frequently the term "Dirge" is applied to these songs, but this seems hardly suitable. *Songs of Sorrow* or *Prayers of Supplication* might better describe them. When harvests fail and earth refuses her increase, or when armies return defeated from the field of battle, a fast-day is proclaimed when the nation humbles itself before its God and seeks renewing grace and power. Thus in Jeremiah 22:1ff. we have an example of such a lament in time of national emergency, and in Joel 2:12–17 we see such a service in full detail. Psalms of this type are 44, 60, 64, 80, 83.

The form and structure are clearly discerned. They begin regularly with a loud cry represented by the name of the deity in the vocative case, *O Jehovah.* This vocative may take us back to far-off times when in polytheistic worship the deity had to be singled out and called by name. Not infrequently that address might be expanded by the addition of honorific epithets, as in the case of the Hymn, so that the opening of the Lament at times resembles the Hymn introduction. Such an invocation is found in Psalm 80.

[9] Eissfeldt, Otto, *Einleitung in das Alte Testament*, p. 123.
[10] Oesterley, W. O. E., *The Psalms*, Vol. I, p. 44.

O shepherd of Israel, give ear,
Thou that leadest Jacob like a flock,
Thou that sittest on the cherubim, shine forth. . . .

But normally it begins, as in Psalm 44, with the simple vocative *O God,* in which is expressed all the passion and urgency of pressing need. After that opening comes 2) the cry for help, followed by a statement of the distressful circumstances into which the suppliants have fallen, and 3) a prayer for help and relief from their calamity. Thus in Psalm 83 we see these separate *motifs* clearly defined:

1. Appeal and introductory cry for help (verse 1)
2. Lament proper setting forth their evil case (verses 2–8)
3. Prayer for Deliverance (verses 9–18)

Frequently there is a setting forth of such comforting thoughts as may confirm faltering faith, and men recall past history to find new hope in their present distress. Thus Psalm 44 opens with the usual address and immediately proceeds to review past history, recounting the great things God hath wrought: thereafter comes the statement as to the calamity and prayer for relief. The various *motifs* may change places at times, but these constituent elements are constant features of the literary structure.

Attention should be called to an additional feature which characterises some of these psalms. We refer to the oracle. In Psalm 60 an oracle occurs, and there is reason to think that such was a usual feature in this type. These songs were in close relation to the religious cult, and it would seem that at a certain point in the ritual act a priest or prophet would give an oracle in answer to the people's prayer. This practice is well-attested in the case of Babylonian psalms, and its existence in Israel's worship seems to be clearly evidenced not only by the Psalter but by the prophetic literature of the Old Testament. It does not appear in all those psalms as we now have them, but it does seem to be present in Psalms 60 and 85, the latter being a liturgy of which the *Community Lament* forms part. It is possible that it was present in their psalms of this type though it is not now represented in our text. The passing from a mood of desperation to a mood of confidence can best be explained by some such procedure. Such dramatic action must have taken place in the cult act. In Psalm 85 we see a people on its knees in a day of national humiliation and prayer, pouring out its heart to God. At verse 8 of the psalm a sudden change takes place and the first personal pronoun appears. This is the oracle spoken by a temple prophet to whom the responsive word of God has come. He rises in his place and all eyes are fixed upon him, all hearts are tense. The Hebrew words in their short staccato phrases reveal the tenseness of the situation:

> I will hear what he says—'tis the Lord—
> Yes, he is speaking to his people—Peace!
> To his saints and those who turn their hearts to
> him.
>
> Yes, soon shall his worshipers see his salvation,
> And glory shall dwell in our land.

When that prophet rose from the kneeling throng all eyes were fixed on him. What will it be? Will it be Peace? Full many an oracle had been given in days gone by by men inspired and all too often their words had sounded like clods falling on coffins, for their message was of judgment and of doom. Would it be that again? God forbid! It is *Peace*! Nothing need be added to that great Hebrew word (*Shalōm*). Peace (*Shalōm*) is one of the most comprehensive words in the Hebrew language and it is as satisfying as it is comprehensive. It signifies wholeness, completeness, soundness, with no deficiency attached, welfare material and spiritual, all debts paid and no scores outstanding, general well-being of body and soul. That is what men longed to hear: it was a word that set all the bells ringing and all the trumpets sounding. This clearly demonstrates the sheer vitality and sense of expectation that characterised Hebrew worship. Their God was the living God and he did things.

Parallels to this procedure in worship may be found in the Old Testament (Judges 7:6–15; 20:26–28; II Kings 19:14–34; II Chronicles 20:3–17). The last reference is peculiarly interesting and relevant, for it concerns an oracle given by a cult prophet on the day of a *Community Lament*. While the congregation is at prayer, in the midst of its passionate plea arises a prophet to speak the responsive word of God in answer to their cry:

> And Jehoshaphat feared and set himself to seek the Lord, and proclaimed a fast throughout all Judah. And Judah gathered themselves together to ask *help* of the Lord: even out of all the cities of Judah they came to seek the Lord. . . . Then upon Jahaziel, the son of Zechariah, the son of Benaiah, a Levite of the sons of Asaph, came the spirit of the Lord in the midst of the congregation; And he said, Hearken ye, all Judah, and ye inhabitants of Jerusalem, and thou, king Jehoshaphat, Thus saith the Lord unto you, Be not afraid nor dismayed by reason of this great multitude; for the battle is not yours, but God's. . . . set yourselves, stand ye still, and see the salvation of the Lord with you, O Judah and Jerusalem. . . . and Jehoshaphat bowed his head with *his* face to the ground, and all Judah and the inhabitants of Jerusalem fell before the Lord, worshiping the Lord.
>
> II CHRONICLES 20:3, 4, 14–18)

That was the way in which the cult functioned in old Israel and we may well believe that something of this is reflected in these psalms. These songs must be interpreted against the living background of the cult and its ritual.

The *Royal Psalms* (2, 18, 20, 21, 45, 62, 101, 110, 132,

144:1–11) concern themselves with the earthly king and have reference to various events in the monarch's career. Psalm 2 deals with the accession and coronation of the king, who is God's Messiah (Anointed). Psalm 45 tells of a royal marriage and may have originated in northern Israel. Psalm 20 deals with the king going forth to war, as does also Psalm 144, while Psalm 18 refers to his return in triumph. Like Psalm 45 this psalm seems to reveal Canaanite influence. Many parallels to these songs are found in Babylon and Egypt, and all are characterised by the "court style" (*Hofstil*) which abounds in huge hyperboles. Such fulsome flattery and exaggerated praise might be in place when applied to the Babylonian and Egyptian imperial conquerors but it is strangely out of place with reference to the kings of little Israel. Israel was of small importance as a military people and played a quite insignificant part in international affairs. But it should be carefully noted that there is here no deification of the king: in the Psalter he is always regarded as the Anointed (Messiah) of Jehovah, and he functions as his representative and servant. For this reason those songs have been generally interpreted in a Messianic sense, though the original reference to the reigning monarch is clear. The question of the later Messianic interpretation will be considered in our exposition of Psalm 2 (p. 197). There is no definite literary form in these songs, as they belong to various types; they fall under *Songs of Thanksgiving* or *Laments*. Most of them belong to the former class.

iii

Gunkel's fourth main type is that of the *Lament of the Individual*. This group constitutes the largest single class in the Psalter and about forty [11] such songs are found in the

[11] Psalms 3, 5, 6, 7, 13, 17, 22, 25, 26, 27:1–14, 28, 31, 35, 38, 39, 42, 43, 51, 54, 55, 56, 57, 59, 61, 63, 64, 69, 70, 71, 86, 88, 102, 109, 120, 130, 140, 141, 142, 143.

book. The range is even wider than that figure would indicate, for many laments occur within the *Mixed Groups*, and the *Psalms of Trust,* or *Confidence,* such as Psalms 4, 11, 16, 23, 27:1–6, 62, 121, find their source and origin here and are derived therefrom. Such a list might suggest that here we find the basic element of the Psalter, for in number they exceed all other groups, and they reveal more intensity and passion than any other type.

That these songs were written by individuals is obvious. The form itself is used by Job and Jeremiah, and even within the psalms the singer is separated and clearly distinguished from the group (Psalm 88:8; 38:25; 22:23). The older interpretation which saw the nation in the individual reference must be set aside: its inadequacy and unreality are clearly seen in such a psalm as 30. Reference may be made here to the interesting conception of *Corporate Personality* in the Old Testament, as worked out by H. Wheeler Robinson.[11] It may be difficult for us to understand what this means, for it is a conception peculiar to the Hebrews. But we observe how sometimes within a psalm (e.g. 44) the first person singular will interchange with the first person plural in a way that seems somewhat bewildering. But it was not bewildering to the Hebrew. Our first thought is of the rights of the individual, but that was not the first thought of the Hebrew: his first thought was of the nation or clan or tribe, and without that thought he could not conceive of an individual at all. The individual to him had no existence apart from the community, but the nation was in the individual, and any Israelite was the nation, for all that pertained to Israel was found in him. Where two or three were gathered together there was Israel, and at times the individual could narrow the thought of the nation to himself (Isaiah 53) or expand himself to include all the people (Psalm 129). "There is," says Robinson, "fluidity

---

[11] *The Old Testament, its Making and Meaning,* p. 85.

of transition from the one to the many, and *vice versa.* Thus the prophet can feel not only that he represents but that he actually is Israel." Here we have a conception that is fruitful in the interpretation of much in the Old Testament though there still remains a residue in the Psalter that seems too individual to be resolved in this fashion: that residue is so personal that we cannot think of anything else than individual writers. Such individual *Laments* abound in the parallels from Babylon and Egypt, and we cannot regard these as other than the expressions of individual worshipers. Let us now look at the literary form and cult background of these psalms.

The *Laments of the Community* were associated with national disasters; the *Lament of the Individual* was associated with personal sickness and suffering. Here man cries "from the depths" because the hand of God is heavy upon him. The oldest form here may have been that of incantation and exorcism; Mowinckel [12] would find numerous traces of the black art in these psalms. The black art must have played its part in primitive life and it may be traces of this can be found in our present Psalter (e.g. Psalm 91), but the psalms as we have them now have passed beyond that stage and must be interpreted in a higher sense. Mowinckel puts too much emphasis on the primitive and fails to allow for the development of ideas. While those *Laments* originated in the cult and the forms in which they were expressed are derived from the cult it would appear that here we are dealing with a main development. For this thing that originated in the cult later moved away from the cult, passing from its point of origin into "spiritual songs" and finally returning in its developed form to enrich and beautify the cult. That raises the question of what the Psalter really is and we must postpone that question for the moment.

The literary form is similar to that of the *Community*

[12] Mowinckel, Sigmund, *Psalmenstudien,* I and V.

Lament. The opening cry to God, the complaint and prayer
for relief are all clearly defined and marked off. It generally
closes with the assurance of being heard and this latter portion of the Lament has given rise to those "Songs of Confidence" to which we have already referred (p. 42). In those
expressions of confident trust we have passed from all the
storm and stress that gave birth to the lament. Oesterley
finds it difficult to accept such an origin for these psalms
but it seems natural and reasonable. When all pain has
turned to peace the singer recalls only the goodness of God
and dwells upon it in this satisfying fashion.

iv

The fifth main group is the *Thanksgiving of the Individual* (18, 30, 32, 34, 40:2–12, 41, 66, 92, 100, 107, 116,
118, 138). There are more such songs for the individual
than for the nation: of the latter we have only two examples (124, 129). The national thanksgiving usually found
expression in the more jubilant *Hymn.* The Song of Thanksgiving has as its dark background the *Lament* and often
these *Laments* conclude with a vow that if God will heal
the sick man and raise him from his bed of pain then the
sick man will offer a certain sacrifice. Both the sacrifice and
the song bear the same Hebrew name, *tōdā*, and the song
accompanies the sacrifice. In Psalm 116 we see the cult
background clearly. Here is a man healed of his sickness
come into the temple, accompanied by his friends, to discharge the vow he had made. We listen as he says:

> I love the Lord, because my voice
> and prayers he did hear.
> I, while I live, will call on him
> who bow'd to me his ear.
> Of death the cords and sorrows did
> about me compass round:

> The pains of hell took hold on me,
>   I grief and trouble found.
>
> Upon the name of God the Lord
>   then did I call and say,
> Deliver thou my soul, O Lord,
>   I do thee humbly pray.

Now that he has come to pay his vow he proceeds to declare that purpose:

> I'll of salvation take the cup,
>   on God's name will I call;
> I'll pay my vows now to the Lord
>   before his people all.
>
> Dear in God's sight is his saint's death
>   thy servant, Lord, am I;
> Thy servant sure, thine handmaid's son;
>   my bands thou didst untie.
>
> Thankofferings I to thee will give,
>   and on God's name will call.
> I'll pay my vows now to the Lord
>   before his people all;
> Within the courts of God's own house,
>   within the midst of thee,
> O city of Jerusalem,
>   praise to the Lord give ye.
>
> (PSALM 116:1–4, 13–19)

It is to be observed that in these *Songs of Thanksgiving* we frequently meet with more harrowing details as to "the descent to hell" than are found in the *Laments*. The reason may well be that it was easier for the psalmist to dwell upon such distressing details in retrospect: the recital of these seems to afford stronger ground for praise and thanksgiving.

The occasion was a private, and not public, feast. The man was accompanied by his friends who were probably entertained by him. It is obvious that such a song could not be composed by him on the spur of the moment. What we have here is a form designed for general use. The worshiper was led in the act of worship by the ministering priest and said the words after the priest just as a man or woman will repeat the words of the Marriage Service after the officiating minister. Harps and lutes might accompany the song (Psalm 43:4; 71:22). The form may be analysed as follows:

1. Introduction
2. Narration: a) recounting of trouble
              b) his call on God
              c) his deliverance
3. Acknowledgment (the root meaning of *tōdā* is to acknowledge)
4. Announcement of thankoffering. In later psalms thanksgiving takes the place of material sacrifice.

It would seem as if the friends of the man took part in the song. Psalms 66 and 118 seem to show responsive singing, while in Psalm 107 various groups in succession take up the tale of thanksgiving. At times the relation between the *Lament* and the *Song of Thanksgiving* becomes very clear, as when, in the latter, the singer recalls words uttered in the *Lament* (Psalm 30:9f.; 31:22; 32:5) or, in the former, when assurance of being heard steals into the *Lament* and the singer passes over to praise. The two types are related "like the halves of a shell" (Gunkel). The relation to the *Hymn* is close, for the note of praise is common to both. In the *Song of Thanksgiving* the singer rejoices over a particular favor granted by God, while in the *Hymn* he sings of God's greatness and his glorious attributes in general. The deprecation of animal sacrifices may be due to prophetic influence (Psalm 40:6; 50:14; 51:16f.), while the influence of the Hebrew sages may be traced in such psalms as 32:8f.; 34:12-15, where the singer seeks to impart wisdom based on his own experience. Psalm 116, which we have just examined, may be regarded as a cult stereotype.

The other types require little notice as the titles are largely self-explanatory. Some of them are so small as to scarcely merit a title. There are but two *Pilgrim Psalms* (84, 122), and two national songs of thanksgiving (124, 129). Psalms dealing with the Law are 1, 15, 24:7–10, 119. Wisdom Psalms are such as concern themselves with the guidance of life (127, 128, 133) or with the deeper problems of human existence (16, 37, 49, 73).

5

"PSALMS AND SPIRITUAL SONGS"

That the psalms are closely associated with the cult and that they originated in the worship of the community is a point on which both Gunkel and Mowinckel are agreed. In this most modern scholars follow them.

> Careful examination will show exactly how various types of psalm were connected with various types of sacrificial worship. For instance, the hymns of thanksgiving were connected with the thank-offerings; the Hebrew word is the same in both cases. This observation suffices to indicate that, if psalms were connected with Israel's sacrificial worship, psalmody was as old as sacrificial worship itself.[1]

We are here dealing with ancient forms of worship and we must be clear as to the ideas lying behind that worship. A great part of the Old Testament is occupied with directions as to the ritual and conduct of worship: the Jew lays great emphasis on all such directions (Hebrew *Tora*, plural *Toroth*). The cult was closely bound up with the life of Israel and we find here, as elsewhere, a body of priests and officials who serve the cult and guide the worshipers in their wor-

[1] Gressmann, Hugo, in *The Psalmists*, edited by D. C. Simpson, p. 9.

ship. The cult must be handled aright and the Deity must
be approached with proper reverence.

> Lord, who shall abide in thy tabernacle?
> Who shall dwell in thy holy hill?
>
> (PSALM 15:1)

Careful and exact directions are required by those who
would enter into the house of God and these directions are
given by the priest or temple official. A war must be sanc-
tified, a house may not be built, a garden cannot be planted
or a marriage celebrated without the proper cult usage and
ritual. Thus for all such and similar acts there were rubrics
in the hands of the priests—the book of Leviticus is almost
entirely a priest's manual of instructions—and *the rubrics
were fixed forms which might not be varied.* Just as a minister today will not celebrate the communion with any form
of words which he may put together, but will use the ritual
appointed by his church, so, and much more so, was it in
ancient Israel. There was a tyranny of form such as we can
hardly understand.

Moreover, these cult actions concerned the people in their
congregational and communal life, and, as those people were
largely illiterate in the early period, the forms were stereotyped and were repeated after the priest. Deuteronomy
26:5–10 shows clearly how this matter was carried through.
There we see a man bringing his gift of first-fruits to the
altar and as he prepares to deposit it the priest makes him
repeat a particular form of words. This was specially necessary, for the formula used in making a presentation to Baal
would be very similar. It was necessary to guard against any
confusion as to the nature of the Deity. The formula here
asserts something vital that has to do with the purity of
Hebrew religion. The form runs thus:

> And thou shalt speak and say before the Lord thy
> God, A Syrian ready to perish *was* my father and

> he went down into Egypt and sojourned there with
> a few, and became there a nation, great, mighty
> and populous. And the Egyptians evil entreated us
> and afflicted us, and laid upon us hard bondage:
> and when we cried unto the Lord God of our
> fathers, the Lord heard our voice and looked on our
> affliction, and our labour, and our oppression; and
> the Lord brought us forth out of Egypt with a
> mighty hand and with an outstretched arm, and
> with great terribleness and with signs and with
> wonders. And he hath brought us to this place,
> and hath given us this land, *even* a land that flow-
> eth with milk and honey. And now I have brought
> the first-fruits of the land which thou, O Lord, hast
> given me.

With these words he deposits the basket on the altar and
worships "before the Lord thy God." This was a prescribed
form of words which did not vary: it was a ritual intended
to call every holy memory to mind and to set in review the
redeeming grace of God.

We have already referred to Psalm 116 as the stereotype
form of the *Song of Thanksgiving,* and here again we have
a form of words that might be used by anyone in the appro-
priate circumstances. That this is not at all fanciful is clear
from Babylonian parallels where we find a space left for
the insertion of the worshiper's name: "I, *A. B.,* will pay my
vow to Marduk." Such forms lack individual or local reference because they are intended for general use.

Another such instance confirming this usage is found in
the case of Hannah (I Samuel 2). Hannah had proffered
a petition and poured out her heart before God: she had
vowed that if she might have a son she would dedicate him
to God's service. Hannah's song, as here given, may not be
the original song, but the fact that such a song was ascribed
to her by the later editor shows plainly that he knew such
a song was the necessary accompaniment of making a vow.
It is precisely this constant cult background that illumines

the psalms and clarifies those ancient songs. The cult act consists not only of something done but of something also said or sung. It is drama and recital. The Lord's Supper is drama and the words that accompany, the Word of Institution (I Corinthians 11:23f.), give meaning to it and are themselves illustrated by it. If it were merely drama we should have the Roman Mass, and for this reason, be it said in passing, the Protestant Reformers ordained that the celebration of the Sacrament should be accompanied by the preaching of the Word that appeals to reason and conscience. In the case of the Lord's Supper the rubrics are fixed and the forms stereotyped. That, of course, does not exclude the possibility that even stereotyped forms may be charged deeply with personal experience and emotion.

If we may use a final example let it be the Levitical benediction as given in Numbers 6:24–26:

> The Lord bless thee, and keep thee;
> The Lord make his face shine upon thee,
>   and be gracious unto thee;
> The Lord lift up his countenance upon thee,
>   and give thee peace.

Here again we see the union of word and action. The priest lifted up his hands and stretched them toward the people as he spoke these words. The words were not mere words: they were charged with energy, and both the priest who blessed and the people who received the blessing believed that in this action or drama something of the soul (*Nephesh*) of the priest passed forth and entered into the souls of the people to enrich and amplify their life. Such is the view of Mowinckel and also of Johannes Pedersen [1] who has made profound research into the psychological background of the Hebrews. We may not think in this way when the benediction is pronounced but the Hebrews did think that way. Other examples may be found throughout the

[1] Israel I–II, pp. 182f.

Old Testament (Deuteronomy 21:7f.; II Kings 13:12f.; Psalm 68:24f.; Psalm 149). The last example is interesting in that it appears to show a sword dance as part of the cult drama.

> Let the saints exult in honor,
> Let them shout in endless joy,
> With exaltation of God in their throats,
> And double-edged swords in their hands.

Worship in ancient Israel was not lacking in vigor and animation and these examples reveal how the cult was rooted in the life of the people. That cult consisted of drama and song, something done and something sung. Where we have the song we can tell the action; where we have the action we can tell the song.

ii

Mowinckel declares that all our psalms in the present Psalter are cult songs of this type. Psalm 1, which is probably a foreword to the Psalter, and Psalm 119, which is the longest psalm, are the only two he finds difficulty in placing in a suitable background of ritual. Recent discoveries, however, in the field of archaeology would suggest that even Psalm 119 may have found its origin in the cult, though most scholars regard it as an academic exercise without any reference to communal worship. Gunkel, on the other hand, holds that the psalms had their origin in the cult, but that psalm-writing later became a matter for the devout individual and that most of the psalms in our Psalter were penned by men who had no thought of the cult or might even be opposed to it. The songs they wrote for their own edification out of their own devotional life might later be taken over into the service of the sanctuary and employed in the cult. This seems more reasonable and in accord with what we find elsewhere in the history of hymnology.

For many of the psalms were written far away from the

temple (42–43). Jonah's psalm (Jonah 2) could hardly be sung with cult accompaniment, and the *Prayer of Manasseh* is by one ostensibly in exile. Nor can we think of Jeremiah's passionate prayers, which assume the form of *Individual Laments,* as associated with the cult. Still less could we imagine Job's wild whirling words to be stereotyped expressions. Nor may we regard the deep inwardness and profound religious insight of such psalms as 51, 103, 104, 139, and many more as springing from a mechanical thing like the cult. The forms are derived from the cult but the deepest tones of the singers are not ready-made or produced by mechanical device. They are too living and vital to be anything but the spontaneous outpouring of individual hearts. Gunkel is right in his strong dissent from the position of Mowinckel, for the latter surely errs in laying such stress on the survival of the primitive. The *Psalms as they have come to us are the religious documents, public and private, of the post-exilic period.* Here is the community that is responsible for the formation of our Old Testament, though the documents which were then assembled and edited may belong to earlier periods. Many traces of the primitive may be found in all these documents, and such traces are not lacking in the Psalter. But it is always dangerous to found theology on etymology, for words grow and develop and their meaning changes with changing time. There is such a thing as development in religion though fossil remains may lie embedded in the language of devotion. Instances may be found in modern hymnals.

> Hobgoblin nor foul fiend
>   can daunt his spirit:
> He knows he at the end
>   shall life inherit.
> Then fancies fly away;
> He'll fear not what men say:
> He'll labor night and day
>   to be a pilgrim.

The Church of Scotland has set that hymn of Bunyan's in its most recent hymnal, but it is very certain that when present day Scots sing these words they do not think of hobgoblins as Bunyan thought. They were very real to him but to us they are no more than poetic figures. Or when we sing Robert Grant's hymn,

> O tell of his might, O sing of his grace,
> Whose robe is the light, whose canopy space.
> His chariots of wrath the deep thunder-clouds form,
> And dark is his path on the wings of the storm,

it may not occur to us that we are using language of pure mythology that once meant to the singers exactly what it says. For us that mythology has faded into poetry and we moralise and spiritualise what earlier men materialised. So it must always be. So, we may be sure, it has been with the *Praises of Israel.*

There are many psalms, too, that had originally no cult reference but are to be received rather as the pious reflections of individual saints. These psalms may have been produced far enough from the temple in synagogues across the seas among the Jews of the Diaspora. Later they found a wider audience and they were probably later adapted to cult usage. Kipling did not write hymns deliberately, but some of his poems, like the "Recessional," have found their place in our hymnals. The verses of Addison and Whittier have shared the same experience. Psalm 30 is a clear example of an individual song that has been later incorporated in the cult and furnished with a cult title. Thus our view of the Psalter will be that it originated first in the cult, from which the forms are derived, that later it passed outside the cult to the homes of the people to become the deposit of their deepest religious life, and that finally it returned, varied and enriched, to beautify the cult and bequeath to us our present book of Psalms.

PART II

TYPES AND INTERPRETATIONS

6

A HYMN OF PRAISE

PSALM 103

BLESS THE LORD, O MY SOUL

1 Bless the Lord, O my soul;
   and all that is within me, *bless* his holy name.

2 Bless the Lord, O my soul,
   and forget not all his benefits:

3 Who forgiveth all thine iniquities;
   who healeth all thy diseases;

4 Who redeemeth thy life from destruction;
   who crowneth thee with loving-kindnesses and tender
      mercies;

5 Who satisfieth thy mouth with good *things*;
   so that thy youth is renewed like the eagle's.

6 The Lord executeth righteousness
   and judgment for all that are oppressed.

7 He made known his ways unto Moses,
   his acts unto the children of Israel.

8 The Lord *is* merciful and gracious,
   slow to anger, and plenteous in mercy.

9 He will not always chide;
   neither will he keep *his anger* for ever.

10 He hath not dealt with us after our sins,
    nor rewarded us according to our iniquities.

11 For as the heaven is high above the earth,
    so great is his mercy toward them that fear him.

12 As far as the east is from the west,
    so far hath he removed our transgressions from us.

13 Like as a father pitieth *his* children,
    so the Lord pitieth them that fear him.

14 For he knoweth our frame;
    he remembereth that we are dust.

15 *As for* man, his days *are* as grass;
    as a flower of the field, so he flourisheth:

16 For the wind passeth over it, and it is gone;
    and the place thereof shall know it no more.

17 But the mercy of the Lord is from everlasting to
    everlasting upon them that fear him,
    and his righteousness unto children's children;

18 To such as keep his covenant,
    and to those that remember his commandments to do
    them.

19 The Lord hath prepared his throne in the heavens;
    and his kingdom ruleth over all.

20 Bless the Lord, ye his angels,
    that excel in strength, that do his commandments,
    hearkening unto the voice of his word.

21 Bless ye the Lord, all *ye* his hosts;
    ye ministers of his, that do his pleasure.

22 Bless the Lord, all his works
    in all places of his dominion:
    bless the Lord, O my soul.

i

The Psalter contains not a few hymns sung by choirs or
congregations, but here we have the hymn of the solitary

soul that aches to express its praise. Here is the product
of personal piety and devotion, a hymn that constitutes
one of the loftiest expressions of individual religion found
in the Old Testament. Staerk remarks rightly: "The poet
of this song of thanksgiving is one of the saints of the Old
Covenant, on whom Christians must look with reverence."
For there is here a profundity of theological view that has
comforted and sustained countless generations. Few psalms
are better known or more beloved. All the evangelical theology is here, for here is present the evangelical experience
in all its fulness. The man who penned this song had known
sickness, and had come near to death, and he had been
overwhelmed with a load of guilt. He had walked in the
valley of the dark shadow, but now he treads the heights
and the sun shines as it never shone before, for God has
been gracious. The poet will hymn the redeeming love
of God.

His experience has given him insight into the real character of God and brought him to an understanding of
the ways of God with his people Israel. To the Hebrew all
history was sacramental. It was the sphere of revelation.
Thus the centerpiece of the poem (verses 6–13) finds the
individual experience confirmed and corroborated in the
larger sphere of Israel's history. Objection has been made
against these verses on the ground that they are somewhat
jejune and conventional, being composed mainly of cita-
tions from the Old Testament. This objection, however,
might be brought against the Lord's Prayer—and it has
been frequently made—whose various sections can be par-
alleled from earlier Jewish teachings. But surely originality
is not to be regarded as the promulgation of ideas wholly
novel, for such would fail to be understood, but rather as
the combination and collocation of truths already established to set them in a new and fresh light. It may concern

also the spirit that informs such combinations and colloca-
tions. Here we are concerned with the interpretation of experience, national and individual, and it is this that constitutes the distinction of the song. Here we have the enuncia-
tion of principles which are based on experience and are
regulative of life at all times. The poet's emphasis on the
fatherly love of God (verse 13), even though that love be
limited to a group within Israel, marks a significant mile-
stone on the way to a fuller revelation of the divine love in
Christ. The advanced theological position, in which the
singer seems indebted to the prophets Hosea, Job, and Isaiah
40–55, would indicate a date for the psalm in the post-exilic
period. That such profound spiritual insight should have
existed in that period alongside the regnant mechanical conceptions of the cult is proof of the sheer vitality of Israel's
religion and the abiding influence of the prophets.

There is a real simplicity about the form of the hymn
and its development of thought. Here we have a natural
development in the way of reflection on the part of a pious
soul who has undergone a transforming and liberating experience. Here is nothing showy or artificial, only the simple
unfolding of truth as the poet has been able to see it. The
summons to praise, addressed to his soul, is followed by a
description of the content of grace as it has been revealed
in his life (verses 3–5). This leads to a survey of national
history which, in its revelation of grace, corroborates and
confirms the individual experience and unfolds the ground
of universal hope (verses 6–13). Thereupon, follows what
might seem a digression in which the brevity of human life
is set over against God's eternity (verses 14–18). But these
verses form no real digression: they are essential to the
poet's thought and are here introduced to magnify the sheer
wonder of the divine grace that condescends to so weak and
frail a creature as man. It is the reverse side of Isaiah's

thought of the exaltedness of God which finds correspond-
ing expression in the thought of the Deuteronomist that
God condescended to make a covenant with Israel, the least
of all the nations. It is the same note of wonder which rings
through all Paul's writings:

> not meet to be called an apostle, because I perse-
> cuted the church of God. But by the grace of God
> I am what I am.
>
>   (I CORINTHIANS 15:9, 10)

That is the surpassing wonder of the divine grace that rivets
and holds the soul of the redeemed. With a further summons he calls upon all beings in heaven and earth to praise,
and finally returns with the renewed summons to his own
soul (verses 19–22).

ii

As already indicated, the song opens with a departure
from the normal form and the singer calls on his own soul
to praise. Here we have not any mechanical thankoffering
but the jubilant upsurge of a heart that knows that all he is
and all he has is due to the grace of God. Reverence and awe
fill the heart that has become conscious of redeeming grace,
and it is precisely this combination of profound awe and
exulting confidence that makes those tones so rich and moving. The Hebrew thought more frequently of the sterner
aspects of Deity, of anger and judgment, but here the "far
God" of Isaiah and the "near God" of Hosea, the God of
terror and judgment and the God whose very heart breaks
for love, meet in this experience of redemption. These two
ideas of God we may hold apart in our thinking, but they
are merged and fused in the real experience of God and his
saving activity. The divine reality is here in all its fulness.
Man in his weakness bows before the righteous God and
finds that judgment is mingled with mercy, that mercy

triumphs over judgment, yea, that the ultimate end of judgment is mercy. That God should bridge the gulf that separates man from Deity, and that he should bridge it in mercy, is an experience that awes the soul, subdues the heart, and constrains to praise and adoration. In that experience God is recognised and known in his real nature and essence as holy redemptive love. The call to the soul is, therefore, no formal matter: it is a summons to realise and remember what life becomes by the grace of God.

It is characteristic of the poet that he begins with the forgiveness of sin (verse 3). By that release the life that was straitened and confined gains new strength and vision. Away from God life could not rise to any amplitude of being. Sickness and impending death, in which the judgment of God was expressed, have passed away. His very weakness has become the point where the divine grace and power are revealed. Now he begins to really live. In verse 5 there may be reference to the fabled phoenix of antiquity, and that same reference may be in the mind of Isaiah of the Exile (Isaiah 40:31): only thus can the poet indicate the greatness of the change wrought in him. To use the language of the New Testament, he is "born again," and life is filled with a strange new joy. For life begins only when it becomes God-filled, and nothing else deserves the name of life.

iii

Here the poet takes a wider sweep. Having looked within his own soul, he now looks out. He will praise God not only for what he has done for his soul: he will praise God for what he has always been, "a just God *and* a Savior." Like the prophets who were overwhelmed with the reality of God, made clear to them in their call and consecration, and knew that such experience might be the portion of all God's people, so the poet here knows that his experience has been the portion of the nation and may yet be the portion of every individual (verses 6, 7). He still sings of judgment and mercy. "The Lord, the Lord God, merciful and gracious, slow to anger and abundant in goodness and truth, keeping mercy to thousands, forgiving iniquity and transgression and sin, and that will by no means clear the guilty." (Exodus 34:6, 7.) Such was the word of Moses in the beginning, and all history has been the explication of that word. With an eye that has been opened to fundamental realities through his transforming experience the poet sees that it has been so with God's redemptive purpose in history as on the more restricted plane of his individual life. Men have failed to see the real nature and character of God, and have formed their doctrines of divine recompense and enunciated narrow theologies. They have concentrated on the divine wrath and failed to see that wrath was but the reverse side of love, the reaction of love against all that injures the objects of his love. It was indeed easier for the Hebrew to think along this line than to see that God's grace is more than man's sin, and his love more than his wrath. It is this distinction the poet has in mind and it his merit that he sees it clearly (verses 8, 9). Something God does keep for ever but that something is not his wrath: it is his love. Sin can be understood only by one who has known the divine grace, the grace that conquers sin and swallows it up and reigns with undisputed dominion. And so, with tender similes and terms of affection, he sets forth the nature of that redeeming grace, the reality and reach of this redemption, beside which man can set nothing in comparison (verses 10–13). It is not within the power of human speech to set forth the fatherly tenderness of God. The repetition in verses 11 and 17 of the words "them that fear him" (literally *his fearers*) conveys the sense of awe and gratitude that fills the mind of the poet. Such knowledge is too high for him: the plummet here falls in fathomless waters. Paul, too, is lost in wonder and praise as he thinks of it:

> O the depth of the riches both of the wisdom
> and knowledge of God! how unsearchable *are*
> his judgments, and his ways past finding out!
>
> (ROMANS 11:33)

iv

In familiar phrases the poet dwells on man's frailty and transiency, but not in the spirit of lamenting despair. Here we have a sentiment akin to that revealed in Psalm 90 where man's weakness is used as a foil to set forth the divine greatness. Here the poet is lingering fondly on the thought of God's wondrous love that condescends to succor and save such poor earth-born creatures. It is because man is so weak and helpless that the divine love is drawn down to his necessity. Divine strength is perfected in human weakness (verses 14–16). Man of himself is nothing: from dust he comes and to dust returns. With many a simile do those Hebrew poets set forth the brevity of life and demonstrate the feebleness of man. It is all so pathetic and it would all be so meaningless were there not something beyond and above to give it meaning. And there is something, there is *Someone* above man's frailty and transiency (verses 17, 18). All our frailty and weakness can be turned to strength and confidence by obedience, according as we lay hold of the covenant promises and find our true life in God.

Finally, because life for him was now set "in the heavenlies" and he knows the full intention of the divine heart, he sets forth the ground of his jubilant confidence in the thought of the kingdom of God. This idea is older than we think, and it lies back of the impregnable faith of the Hebrew.

> The Lord—in heaven he hath set his throne,
> and his kingdom ruleth over all.
>
> (VERSE 19)

That is the ground of hope for all mankind, and in view of it the poet finds words too weak to bear the weight of his gratitude and praise. Thus he calls on all the hosts of heaven to share his joy and lend elevation to his song (verses 20–22).

Thus amid all these crashing harmonies the poet returns to where he began, "the Lord, the Lord God, merciful and gracious." This is the alpha and omega of his song and like a golden circlet he completes it with the new and never-ending summons to his own soul:

Bless the Lord, O my soul.

7

A SONG OF ZION

PSALM 46

EIN FESTE BURG IST UNSER GOTT

1   God *is* our refuge and strength,
    a very present help in trouble.

2   Therefore will not we fear, though the earth be removed, and though the mountains be carried into the midst of the sea;

3   *Though* the waters thereof roar *and* be troubled,
    though the mountains shake with the swelling thereof.

4   *There is* a river, the streams whereof make glad the city of God,
    the holy place of the tabernacles of the Most High.

5   God *is* in the midst of her; she shall not be moved:
    God shall help her, *and that* right early.

6   The heathen raged, the kingdoms were moved:
    he uttered his voice, the earth melted.

7   The Lord of hosts is with us;
    the God of Jacob is our refuge.

8   Come, behold the works of the Lord,
    what desolations he hath made in the earth.

9 He maketh wars to cease unto the end of the earth;
   he breaketh the bow, and cutteth the spear in sunder;
   he burneth the chariot in fire.

10 Be still, and know that I *am* God:
   I will be exalted among the heathen,
   I will be exalted in the earth.

11 The Lord of hosts is with us;
   the God of Jacob is our refuge.

This psalm may be called the *Hymn of Faith* as I Corinthians 13 is called the *Hymn of Love*. But while it is born of a great faith and has inspired Luther's great battle hymn of the Reformation, *Ein feste Burg ist unser Gott,* which, uniquely enough, is even more vigorous than the original, the question of the original background is far from clear. Older commentators treated the psalm as originating in some great and signal deliverance from Israel's foes through the marvelous intervention of her God. Nothing, indeed, could be more natural than to think of such an origin for this psalm, for the Hebrew writes his finest lyrics with his eye upon the subject. Occasions enough there were in Hebrew history when such a song might rise spontaneously from the singer's lips. Miriam at the Sea of Reeds (Exodus 15:20, 21) and Deborah on the plain of Jezreel (Judges 5) come to mind in this connection, and numerous other examples suggest themselves. Israel was a singing people and here surely was occasion for song. Thus scholars found no difficulty in seeing here the jubilation of the nation in presence of the Lord's signal deliverance of Jerusalem from Sennacherib in the year 701 B.C., when

> the Assyrian came down like the wolf on the fold
> and his cohorts were gleaming in purple and gold
>   (Byron, "Destruction of Sennacherib"),

and King Hezekiah was shut up "like a bird in a cage" within his own city. In those days the regal prophet Isaiah was exercising his lofty ministry in Jerusalem and the singer's

repeated phrase, "the Lord of hosts is with us," is strongly
reminiscent of the prophetic watchword *Immanuel* (Isaiah
7:14). If we seek a historical background, there can surely
be none more suitable than this, and it may be that this
glowing, surging hymn was penned by one of Isaiah's immediate disciples under the direct impact of that wondrous
event. Wellhausen thinks the psalm may refer to events in
the Greek period and be concerned with the invasion of
Alexander the Great but this does not seem probable. The
traditional interpretation which assigns it to the Assyrian
invasion of 701 B.C. has much in its favor, and, if a historical
event is sought for basis, none is more satisfying than this.

But another interpretation is possible, and even more
probable, and it is along this line we shall proceed in our
exposition of the psalm. Gunkel and Kittel, to name only
two commentators on the Psalms, both treat the psalm as
an eschatological piece, and refer it not to any historical
event but rather to the final issue of things when *the day of
the Lord* dawns. This line of approach gives a more adequate
interpretation and accords better with the language used
and the ideas expressed in the psalm. The Hebrew tenses
may refer to deliverance past or future, for it was the custom of the prophets to refer to God's intentions and purposes in the past tense. With God to will and to do were
one and the same thing, and the prophet normally regards
these acts not as lying in the future but as already achieved
and behind him. On the ground of grammatical usage no
objection can be made against the eschatological interpretation, for the tenses may be construed as past or future. So
far as the text itself is concerned either interpretation, historical or eschatological, is justified.

i

Gunkel has shown the wide influence of the prophets on
the Psalmists, and that is easily observed throughout the

Psalter. The ethical emphasis in Psalm 15 and the spiritual character of worship revealed in Psalms 51 and 19:14 need only be referred to in order to show that the prophetic seed had fallen in good ground. A great part of the prophetic heritage was eschatology, and the Psalmists entered into that heritage of living faith and vital hope. The present psalm may not be as early as 701 B.C., for sufficient time must be allowed for the prophetic influence to spread and make itself felt. Weiser would prefer to explain the psalm as originating in the historic experience of a great deliverance and only later expanding into an eschatological hymn. He would thus combine the historical and eschatological interpretations, and there is much to be said for this view. The hymn will thus have found its point of origin in a historical happening, for, after all, eschatology and the terms in which it finds expression must have some contact with reality as we know it. While this historical happening may have been in the original writer's mind—for hope is not born *in vacuo*—the song in its final form is giving expression to something that is wholly future and without the scope of history. The psalm in its present form is an eschatological song.

Now, these eschatological songs are often confusing, for the singers frequently operate with old mythological ideas which are largely of alien origin. These ideas originate mainly in Babylon and may have passed, in modified form, into Canaan where the Hebrews found them. They underlie the story of Creation in Genesis 1, and their origin is plain to see, for in that story we find words like *tohu wavohu* (waste and void) and *tehom* (the deep, Babylonian *Tiamat*) taken straight over from the Babylonian story. Those same myths recur, in more or less faded form, in Job (26:5, 12; 38:11) and in the Psalter elsewhere (65:7, 89:9; 93:3; 104:6) and throughout the prophetic books. These ideas were common property and though the prophets use them

only as symbols and poetic figures it must be borne in mind
that common people may have ascribed to them a greater
degree of reality. Indeed the tragedy of the Hebrew prophets seems to lie right here that they were interpreted and
understood literally when they were speaking figuratively.
Many people, ancient and modern, are unable to understand
poetry and must for ever be turning it into prose. In describing future things men cannot but use current terms. John in
his Apocalypse will describe the golden city in finite earthly
terms and the infinite glories are set forth in our mortal
speech. Pavements of glass and seas of fire and streets of
gold may be only symbols and imagery to the mystic John,
but they are all too frequently very real to John's disciples.
They constitute for them the ultimate reality. It would
seem that not only for the Hebrew, but also for the Christian, salvation has very strong material associations. In
like manner when the Old Testament speaks of the new age
it describes it in terms of the original Paradise with rivers
of water and trees of life and the abiding presence of God.
John does not do otherwise in his final view of the New
Jerusalem (Revelation 22:1f.). In the final issue when God's
grace has had its perfect work Paradise Lost will become
Paradise Regained. This is the viewpoint of the present
song.

ii

The song opens like Psalm 11 with a statement of the
national faith. History to the Hebrew was sacramental, for
it revealed and mediated God. History has shown God to be

a help in troubles proved full well

(VERSE 1).

Because of what the Lord has been and because of what he
has done Israel feels strangely fortified and confident. Her
God is Lord, and if God be for us he is more than all that

be against us. With such a God and such a refuge and stronghold man may never need to fear those Messianic woes that must precede the ushering in of God's new and final order (*cp.* Mark 13:13–17). For the birth of the new age, according to popular expectation, was to be attended with fearful signs in heaven above and earth beneath.

> The earth shall quake before them; the heavens shall tremble: the sun and the moon shall be dark, and the stars shall withdraw their shining:
> And the Lord shall utter his voice before his army; for his camp is very great: for *he is* strong that executeth his word: for the day of the Lord *is* great and very terrible; and who can abide it?
> (JOEL 2:10, 11)

When these signs appear men will know that God is moving and that his judgments are about to be set in the earth. That day will mark the beginning of the end of the old order and the initiation of the new age. The Psalmist here is looking to that future time and describing it. As it was in the beginning (*Urzeit*) so shall it be again in the end (*Endzeit*). The Lord will strike into history to end the present chaos and set up his kingdom of good order. The wild chaotic monster of the vasty deep must again be subdued and cosmos evoked from chaos. In that struggle all Nature will be convulsed and dislocated, hills sinking into the sea and earth rent with quaking, but the end is sure. Faith will find its victory, for

> the Lord of hosts is with us,
> the God of Jacob is our refuge.

This refrain occurs at verse 7 and verse 11, and, by inserting it after verse 3, we have something like a regular strophic structure. The refrain may have been sung by the congregation, the priest or choir singing the song itself. In that sense the song would be liturgical. Undismayed by the huge cataclysms of Nature the poet rejoices in all the chaotic upsurge,

for his God is at work and will triumph in the fight. The
Stoic with his resignation never knew the lofty Hebrew
faith that sings when worlds fall apart. The Hebrew saw
through these things to victory, but the Stoic could only
accept them "in accordance with Nature." Moreover, the
old mythological features here are set in the framework of
monotheistic faith. "The Lord alone shall be exalted in that
day" (Isaiah 2:11, 17). Once again the Lord will make a
cosmos and chaos shall be no more. When Nature breaks
beneath his feet man knows that the Lord is there, and that
out of the welter and confusion he will bring forth a new
and nobler order of things.

iii

In the second strophe (verses 4–7) the writer passes to
another feature of the last time. This, too, was characteristic
of the last time, the final wind-up of earthly things, and
Ezekiel has made us familiar with it—the assault of the
heathen peoples upon Jerusalem (Ezekiel 38:1ff.). Gog and
Magog with all their terrifying hosts and their hot devour-
ing appetites will come, but they will assuredly be broken.
As God lives, they shall not stand. For Jerusalem is the
throne of God's glory, "the habitation of the Highest." The
word *holy* in Hebrew originally signified "set apart or reserved for a particular purpose." Zion is reserved and set
apart for Jehovah. This is not exactly Isaiah's doctrine of
the inviolability of Zion: it may include that, but it includes
something more, for here the very being and character of
Israel's God are involved. Here we meet those figures of the
old mythology: God's city is the garden city of Eden with
its fabled river, and from this place flows a stream of
blessing. The psalm may have been composed at some
northern sanctuary such as Dan, where a real river could
be found, and was later incorporated in the *Praises of Israel,*

and sung at the temple of Jerusalem. There was no river in Jerusalem; its water supply was a constant source of worry to those who had to defend the city in time of war (Isaiah 7:3). But there was a river of divine grace, and often did the Hebrew bards sing of it.

> Thine eyes shall see Jerusalem a quiet habitation
> . . . a place of broad rivers and streams
>
> (ISAIAH 33:20, 21)

> Afterward he brought me again unto the door of the house, and behold waters issued out from the threshold eastward . . . and the waters came from under the right side of the house at the south side of the altar.
>
> (EZEKIEL 47:1)

> In the midst of the street of it, and on either side of the river was there the tree of life . . . and the leaves of the tree were for the healing of the nations.
>
> (REVELATION 22:2)

That is how the Hebrews thought of the Holy City, and we need not grudge them those imaginative flights. Nor, on the other hand, need we turn their poetry into prose. The ideas with which the poet is operating are clear enough. As of old the darkness fled before the coming of the light, when God uttered his voice, so here again the golden morn breaks over a world renewed, and Jehovah alone is exalted in that day. Again the triumphant refrain breaks forth, for neither the wild upsurge of ancient chaos nor the rage of heathen peoples will prevail against him (verses 6, 7).

iv

"Come and see." For there is no cure for prejudice but experience. And in this strophe the poet offers ocular demonstration and declares the purpose of it all. For all that has gone before is not the end of things: it is but the beginning

Destruction precedes construction, and all this destructive power is revealed for a constructive purpose. The broken implements of war lie at the end of the way, but they mark the entrance to a new way which man must walk if he would arrive at the City of God. For the final stage must be the age of peace, and that not only by way of release for a war-weary world. The prophet Isaiah had dreamed that same dream:

> Behold the mountain of the Lord
> > In latter days shall rise
> On mountain tops above the hills,
> > And draw all wondering eyes.
>
> . . . . .
>
> The beam that shines from Zion's hill
> > Shall lighten every land:
> The King who reigns in Salem's towers
> > Shall all the world command.
>
> . . . . .
>
> No strife shall rage nor hostile feuds
> > Disturb those peaceful years;
> To ploughshares men shall beat their swords,
> > To pruning-hooks their spears.
>
> No longer host encount'ring hosts
> > Shall crowds of slain deplore:
> They hang the trumpet in the hall,
> > And study war no more.
>
> (ISAIAH 2:1, 3, 5, 6; Scots paraphrase)

Again and again this dream recurs, and it comes with those mythological features; the *Endzeit* will be as the *Urzeit*. Paradise Lost will become Paradise Regained. The same prophet sets that same thought forth in novel form in Isaiah 11:6–9:

> And the wolf shall dwell as guest with the lamb,
> And the leopard shall have the same lair as the kid;

> And the lion shall eat straw like the ox,
> And the calf and the young lion will graze to-
> gether;
> With a little child acting as their driver.
> The cow and the bear shall be companions to
> one another,
> Together shall their young make their lair:
> And the suckling shall play over the hole of
> the asp,
> And over the dwelling of the viper shall the
> weaned child trip about.[1]

That is not born of war-weariness, nor is it the mere longing for peace and rest. It is something far more positive and decisive. It is born of a passion for, and belief in, the kingdom of God wherein men will be subject to him, and his will shall be done and his kingdom established on earth. "In his will is our peace." The final purpose of it all is that he may reign whose right it is to reign (verse 10). "Castles must first be built in the air before cottages can be built on the ground." So wrote David Livingstone from darkest Africa to his sister in Scotland. Dreams and visions must come stealing to the heart and ideals must lay their spell upon the spirit of man before deeds come from his hand or words from his lips. And so we take that ancient dream to our hearts in this distressful time. For here is a faith that overcomes the world, the faith that we have a God big enough to make a new world and good enough to make it a Christian world. And so the final refrain may sound to us an even louder note of triumph:

> the Lord of hosts is with us:
> The God of Jacob is our refuge.

[1] Translated by G. B. Gray in *Isaiah, Inter. Crit. Comm.*

8

A LAMENT OF THE COMMUNITY

PSALM 44

RELIGION IN THE INTERROGATIVE MOOD

1 We have heard with our ears, O God,
   our fathers have told us
   what work thou didst in their days,
   in the times of old.

2 *How* thou didst drive out the heathen with thy hand,
   and plantedst them;
   how thou didst afflict the people,
   and cast them out.

3 For they got not the land in possession by their own
      sword,
   neither did their own arm save them;
   but thy right hand and thine arm and the light of thy
      countenance,
   because thou hadst a favour unto them.

4 Thou art my King, O God:
   command deliverances for Jacob.

5 Through thee will we push down our enemies;
   through thy name will we tread them under that rise
      up against us.

6 For I will not trust in my bow,
   neither shall my sword save me.

7 But thou hast saved us from our enemies,
   and put them to shame that hated us.

8 In God we boast all the day long
   and praise thy name for ever.

9 But thou hast cast us off, and put us to shame,
   and goest not forth with our armies.

10 Thou makest us to turn back from the enemy;
   and they which hate us spoil for themselves.

11 Thou hast given us like sheep appointed for meat;
   and hast scattered us among the heathen.

12 Thou sellest thy people for nought,
   and dost not increase *thy wealth* by their price.

13 Thou makest us a reproach to our neighbors,
   a sport and a derision to them that are round about us.

14 Thou makest us a byword among the heathen,
   a shaking of the head among the people.

15 My confusion *is* continually before me,
   and the shame of my face hath covered me.

16 For the voice of him that reproacheth and blasphemeth;
   by reason of the enemy and avenger.

17 All this is come upon us: yet have we not forgotten
      thee,
   neither have we dealt falsely in thy covenant.

18 Our heart is not turned back,
   neither have our steps declined from thy way.

19 Though thou hast sore broken us in the place of
      dragons,
   and covered us with the shadow of death.

20 If we have forgotten the name of our God
   or stretched out our hands to a strange god;

21   Shall not God search this out?
      for he knoweth the secrets of the heart.

22   Yea, for thy sake we are killed all the day long:
      we are counted as sheep for the slaughter.

23   Awake, why sleepest thou, O Lord?
      arise, cast *us* not off for ever.

24   Wherefore hidest thou thy face,
      and forgettest our affliction and our oppresion?

25   For our soul is bowed down to the dust:
      our belly cleaveth to the earth.

26   Arise for our help,
      and redeem us for thy mercies' sake.

It may not be possible, as Burke says, to bring an indict-
ment against a nation, but the ancient Hebrew people were
at times peculiarly conscious of their national unity. At such
times they could even think of themselves as a single individual and use, as in this present song, the first personal
pronoun. This is that thought of *Corporate Personality* to
which we have already made reference and it is a way of
thought far removed from our ways of thinking. In this
Community Lament we see a people on its knees, wholly
prostrate on the ground. In the expressive phrase of verse 25,

      our belly cleaveth to the earth,

we see the measure of their national humiliation and the
greatness of their grief. In this desperate condition they seek
unto the Lord, for only in him have they any hope. In some
ways the psalm may appear to be set on a rather low level,
and the closing prayers (verses 23–26) with its extreme
urgency and insistency might well offend aesthetic and religious feeling. But it may well be that we ourselves have
never learned to pray as we should, and if those notes of
insistency and urgency were imported into our devotional
services we might begin to get somewhere. Our Lord has
told us of the importunate widow who, with something like

the method of the mosquito, was able to get her will of the
unjust judge (Luke 18:3f.), and while that may not represent the soul of true prayer it surely does represent an element in all prayer that prevails. Moses prayed so:

> Oh this people have sinned a great sin and have
> made them gods of gold! Yet now, if thou wilt for-
> give their sin—and if not, blot me out, I pray thee,
> out of the book which thou hast written.
>
> (EXODUS 32:31, 32)

Jeremiah prayed in the same way (Jeremiah 14:21) and
John Knox cried with the same passion in the days of the
Reformation: "God give me Scotland, or I die." This psalm
may teach us something of the nature of true prayer.

The psalm is frequently assigned to the Maccabean period,
and, if there are psalms in the Psalter from that late time,
this surely might be one of them. But despite very ancient
tradition in regard to the Maccabean origin of this psalm
there seems good reason to question the tradition. It is
doubtful if any psalms in our Psalter originate in a period
as late as that of the Maccabees (165–37 B.C.). Both Gunkel
and Oesterley would deny the presence of such psalms in
our collection. Kittel, on the other hand, accepts the tradition and dates the present psalm in the period of the Maccabees, while Schmidt would assign to it a date in the Persian
period (538–331 B.C.). The history of the Old Testament
canon seems to support those who deny the presence of
Maccabean psalms in our Psalter. The references within the
present song can be interpreted very well with reference to
the period of the Maccabees, but they can also find a satisfying explanation in the history of earlier periods. These
points will become clear in the course of our exposition of
the psalm. The date in the Persian period suggested by
Schmidt offers a period in the national history which might
well correspond to that indicated by the contents of the

psalm. From the viewpoint of history we know more about
the Maccabean period than about the Persian period, but
oppression and persecution such as is here described were
not confined or limited to any special period of history. In
that Persian period life was poor and mean, and the circumstances of the exiles, who had returned so full of hope
in 538 B.C., were highly unfavorable. It may be this is the
situation reflected in verse 19. Altogether it was a depress-
ing time when faith was solely tried and men had good
grounds for calling upon the righteous God to intervene
and set them free with a large release.

i

The psalm begins, as all such psalms begin, with a loud
outcry. *O God*, he cries, for vain is the help of man. None
but the great God can remedy a situation so desperate. All
the passion and pathos of affliction weight that cry with
fulness of meaning. It was customary in such *Laments* to set
forth such comforting thoughts of God as might fortify and
strengthen trembling hearts. Thus we have a somewhat
lengthy exordium reminiscent of the style of the hymn. In it
the poet sets forth such thoughts and brings past history
under review. Faith that trembles confirms itself by appeal
to experience, for history to the Hebrew was full of God.
Thus as the passionate cry, *O God*, breaks from his lips all
that God has been and all that God has done comes to mind,
and he lingers over it. For the reading of history and the
recalling of past events should be an invigorating tonic to
the mind and a reinforcement to the heart that is depressed.
But, on the other hand,

Sorrow's crown of sorrow is remembering happier things.
                              (TENNYSON, *Locksley Hall*)

The memory of the past may only accentuate the agony of
the present time. But for one brief moment his wild outcry

is stilled, but only for a moment, as he sets in array all those righteous acts of the redeeming God who had made Israel a people and given them a land (verse 3). "Had not the Lord been on our side" (Psalm 124:2) it might have been altogether otherwise, but he had gone out with their armies and created victory for them. That all seems so distant now, but faith will lay hold of the promises. For grief and sorrow are so pressing, and the parlous state of the nation brooks no delay. Thus the *Lament* (verses 9–16) follows, in which is described their evil situation. Thereupon follows those considerations which are urged by the people upon their God to induce him to swift remedial action and intervention (verses 17–22). The psalm closes with vigorous petition that almost shocks us by its impetuous violence (verses 23–26).

ii

The opening cry of the group known as *Laments* is always the divine name in the vocative form. Probably here the original was "Jehovah," the covenant name of Israel's God. That name was full of gracious memories and it was the inspiration of Israel's hope. We might infer from the opening that those memories were living memories: it was not something they had read in a book or Bible but the treasury of devout story that fathers had passed on to their sons (verse 1), tales of redemption and victory that the covenant God had bestowed upon his chosen people. That very name now seemed to mock their present distress. Had God ceased to be gracious? "My God, my God, why?", "How long, O Lord, how long?"—these are the common cries in these *Laments*. No nation had a loftier national pride, and, because of Jehovah's goodness to them and his favor to their fathers, they had been "the cynosure of all eyes," and the envy of the nations—but now! They who had sat so high are brought very low, and they are filled with shame (verses

9–12). This also cometh from Jehovah of hosts but it was hard for the people to understand. They saw no Gospel hid in their suffering but only ground for complaint. It seemed irrational that Jehovah should act in this fashion, for not only did he gain nothing by it: he was actually the loser. For his honor was impugned and his fair name aspersed among the heathen. God seemed dead or asleep, and their foes might well say, "Where is now thy God?" The pious Hebrew felt that way himself, but faith remained amid the ruins, and that is why we have this psalm. It is faith in the interrogative mood. Physical suffering might be endurable, but that a proud people like the Jews should be subjected to scorn and contumely of "lesser breeds without the law" was something they did not bear with equanimity. It cut them to the quick that a mongrel race like the Samaritans or half-bred upstarts like the Edomites should be laughing and gloating over their suffering (verses 13, 14). "Ichabod," the glory is departed, and Israel sits disconsolate. Taunts and reproaches, the wagging of heads by leering, jeering folk —these the Jews were called upon to endure, the proud Jews, "whose are the Law and the Prophets." And now they are forced to hang their heads for very shame (verses 15, 16).

iii

Here follows something that is not unusual in such psalms —the protestation of innocence. Such a protestation may not commend itself to us who believe that "by the works of the Law no flesh shall be justified." This expression (verses 17–22) savors too much of what we call Pharisaism, and we have no place for any doctrine that would make the divine salvation depend on human works. "By grace are ye saved, and that not of yourselves: it is the gift of God." But we need not condemn it out of hand. We should rather seek to understand what is involved here. The righteousness of God

is involved, as may be gathered from the wild whirling cries
that have been uttered earlier. The righteousness of God is
involved also in the book of Job, and the issues at stake are
not small. For religion in Job's day, and in the Psalmist's
day, was something simpler than with us: it consisted in
doing things, the things prescribed by the Law. Job could
point proudly to the keeping of this law (Job 31), and the
Psalmist does the same. They hold the record in the face of
God and demand fulfillment of the bond. "Shall not the
Judge of all the earth do right?" He cannot let the good man
suffer or the righteous nation be oppressed. If such a state
of things should come about, surely the divine righteousness
will be challenged, as Job challenges it, or man must recon-
cile himself to the presence of moral anomalies in a world
ruled by a righteous God. To the Old Testament the latter
attitude is impossible. For the Old Testament, by and large,
has no thought of a future world where the injustices of this
present world shall be righted. Things must be put right
here and now. There is no "sweet by-and-by" for the Old
Testament saint. Thus we have these psalms and these
mighty protestations.

But with us *religion does not consist in doing but in being.*
The ethic of the clean heart is more than the ethic of the
thing done. The writer of the 51st Psalm gets closer to this
view, but the 51st Psalm is exceptional. It does not represent the main body of Hebrew piety. The other side of this
matter may be observed in those psalms where beneath the
chastening rod of God a man bethinks himself of what he
has done or left undone, and proceeds to confess his sin. For
the suffering that comes to a man because of his sin can only
be uplifted and taken away by the divine forgiveness. It is
to be noted in this connection that the removal of disease
and pain accompanies the inflow of peace to the troubled
conscience. The singer here is taking his stand as a child
before its father. The child does not expect chastisement for

obedience, and if chastisement comes the child is faced with a painful situation. That is precisely where the singer stands in the present instance. He has a case and we must not overlook those elements in it.

Gunkel would emend the text of verse 19 to read thus:

> Thou hast smitten us like the dragon
> And covered us with gloomy darkness.

This has the merit of presenting a clear image derived from ancient mythology. The reference would then be to the primeval conflict of God with the great serpent, and a parallel to this is found in Job 7:12:

> Am I a sea, or a sea-monster,
> That thou settest a watch over me?

Here the singer is saying that God has beaten down and crushed his people as once he crushed and beat down the great dragon, and cast it into the gloomy darkness. This alteration entails little change in the consonantal text, but we need not accept it. The expression may be due to poetic fancy that was wont to think of deserted places as "the haunt of the bittern" or the abode of jackals. We have retained the text as it stands, and it yields an intelligible idea.

A covenant requires two parties to its making, and, if one has kept the terms and the agreement is ineffectual, then the fault must be in the other party to the agreement. There is here (verses 20, 21) something of the violence of Job though it is not expressed as vehemently. Nevertheless, the argument by suggestion may be forceful enough, and it is so here. There is something irrational and unrighteous in the attitude of God. The age of idolatry for Israel was past. The Exile with its iron discipline had purged the nation's soul, and there was no more "going up on every high hill and under every green tree to commit adultery." Their suffering would be understandable if things were as they once had been, but all that is past, and a righteous people who keep

the Law to the last syllable are being made to "suffer all the
penalties of the damned." The singer comes right out with
it in verse 22:

> Yea, because of thee we are slain all the day long:
> We are counted as sheep for the slaughter.

Many scholars would interpret this verse as referring to
the religious persecutions that occurred in the Maccabean
period when warring sects sought to excommunicate each
other and did not refrain from murder. But such reference
is not sufficient here. Something wider and larger is implied,
and the wider reference suits the context of the psalm. The
Jews were hated and persecuted because of their religion,
and the lofty ethic, that commended itself to men throughout the world, provoked the enmity of baser souls. For a
spiritual religion has always a harder course to run than one
rooted in physical nature. In the same way Christianity
stirred not only the opposition of Judaism but of the whole
pagan world. Sinful men could do nothing with its Founder
but affix him to a cross, for he stood for something that
could not be fitted into the accepted scheme of things. That
is what is emerging here in the present song, though the
singer did not see clearly all that was involved. His religion
had no idea of a cross or of a theology that would center
around a cross. Religion must, he felt, ensure health and
prosperity, and his complaint is that it is not functioning in
the way it should. It is easy to observe from all this what
a history religion has had, and how it has grown from more
to more. This passage is quoted by Paul (Romans 8:36),
but Paul is there sounding depths this singer could not
fathom. The well is deep and he has nothing to draw with.

iv

Had the psalmist been able to see things from the viewpoint of the Apostle, he and his people would have rejoiced

with joy unspeakable that they were counted worthy to
suffer for the sake of Jehovah and his kingdom. They would
have rejoiced in tribulation, knowing well that if they had
fellowship in his sufferings, they would also have fellowship
in his glory. But the Jew could not think that way; the
fuller light had not yet come. Prosperity is the blessing of
the Old Testament but adversity is the blessing of the New
Testament. We must bear in mind those fundamental differences of background, and do justice to this singer. That
which was cause of rejoicing to the New Testament saint
was cause of pain and bewilderment to the Old Testament
pious one. "My God, my God, why?" he cries while Paul
shouts, "Thanks be unto God." The psalmist knew that it
was because he had the God he worshipped, and because he
fulfilled the lofty moral demands which that God laid upon
him and his, that he was exposed to the hatred and scorn of
heathen folk. It is God's own concern, and God must do
something about it. The worshiper is not slow to make that
clear to Jehovah. And so we have that vigorous, violent,
vital prayer that startles us with its almost irreverent
speech. It should be translated with a certain forcefulness
thus:

> Wake up! why sleepest thou, O Lord?
> Awake! Spurn us not for ever.
> Why dost thou hide thy face,
> And forget our misery and oppression?
> For our soul is bowed to the dust,
> And our belly cleaves to the earth.
> Stand up! and be a help to us,
> And redeem us for thy mercy's sake.
>
> (*Verses* 23–26)

The word "mercy" in verse 26 is the familiar Hebrew
Chesed which signifies many things but fundamentally the
bond of loyalty and truth that exists between two parties to
a covenant. Without *Chesed* (mercy, loving-kindness) a cov-

enant cannot be made. The singer is taking his stand on God's pledged word, and that gives him the right to pray as he does. Thus Jeremiah can pray likewise:

> Do not abhor us, for thy name's sake;
> Do not disgrace the throne of thy glory;
> Remember, break not thy covenant with us.
> (JEREMIAH 14:21)

"Would that all the Lord's people were prophets" (Numbers 11:29), and would that we had such vigor and purpose in our prayers. For surely so our prayers would rise from the floor and fly right through the roof straight up to God's own heaven. Such prayers the Father will not deny "for his mercy's sake." Truly "the prayer of a righteous man availeth much *when it is energised.*" [2] Lord, teach us so to pray!

[2] This seems the required translation of James 5:16.

9

A ROYAL PSALM

PSALM 2

THE LORD AND HIS ANOINTED

1 Why do the heathen rage,
and the people imagine a vain thing?

2 The kings of the earth set themselves,
and the rulers take counsel together,
against the Lord and his Anointed, *saying,*

3 Let us break their bands asunder,
and cast away their cords from us.

4 He that sitteth in the heavens shall laugh:
the Lord shall have them in derision.

5 Then shall he speak unto them in his wrath,
and vex them in his sore displeasure.

6 Yet have I set my King
upon my holy hill of Zion.

7 I will declare the decree:
the Lord hath said unto me, Thou art my Son,
this day have I begotten thee.

8   Ask of me, and I shall give *thee*
    the heathen for thine inheritance,
    and the uttermost parts of the earth for thy possession.

9   Thou shalt break them with a rod of iron:
    thou shalt dash them in pieces like a potter's vessel.

10   Be wise now therefore, O ye kings;
    be instructed, ye judges of the earth.

11   Serve the Lord with fear,
    and rejoice with trembling.

12   Kiss the Son, lest he be angry,
    and ye perish *from* the way,
    when his wrath is kindled but a little.
    Blessed *are* all they that put their trust in him.

This psalm belongs to the group of Royal Psalms. It is concerned with one of Israel's kings, who, being anointed with the holy oil, is called *the Lord's Messiah,* Messiah being the Hebrew word for anointed as *Christos* (Christ) is the Greek word. The poem may have been composed by the poet laureate of the period: that poet may have been one of the court prophets whom we meet frequently enough in the Old Testament. The poem would seem to have been written on the occasion of the king's coronation in precisely the same way as such a coronation ode was written by the poet laureate of Britain on the accession of the present monarch. There would be, on such an occasion, no limit to what the poet might say, and, however extravagant the terms used may seem to us, they find numerous parallels in Egyptian and Babylonian psalms of similar character. It is written in "court style," and it is precisely this feature that has led most commentators to call these songs Messianic psalms. For they felt that such language could not be used of any of the sons of men, and, therefore, they interpreted the whole group (2, 18, 20, 21, 45, 72, 101, 110, 132, 144: 1–11) with reference to Christ. Such reference may be—and can be—justified, but a sound exegesis must begin with the original reference: in doing so we may win a fuller justification for the Messianic reference. Those earlier commentators failed to take note of the Oriental court style, and they failed to observe that the Oriental naturally indulges in huge hyperbole.

i

Scholars are divided in opinion as to the number of speakers in the poem. Both Mowinckel and Kittel regard it as a liturgical psalm in which several actors take part, and the poem can easily be divided, in dramatic form, between king, poet, and Jehovah. But it seems preferable, and more natural, to suppose that there is but one speaker throughout and he is the poet who composed the ode. It might be possible, also, to think of the king himself reciting the ode which his poet laureate had composed, but this seems less natural. The poem is written with great dramatic power, and straightway we are ushered into the midst of things, and hear and see the vast commotion of assembled hosts. They are setting the stage for a "showdown." The word used in the second verse for "meditate" is the same word as is used in Psalm 1 of the godly man musing over his Bible. Here there is something more than musing or humming; what we have here is a fierce muttering by men who plan some great evil.

Such occurrences as are here described were common enough in ancient history. The Old Testament gives many instances of this common phenomenon. Whenever one of those great military colossi died such movements as this were the usual occurrence. The subject states that chafed under oppression and tyranny were thirsting for the chance

to rebel, and the death of the great tyrant was the signal for
uprisings throughout his empire. For those empires were not
bound together by any spiritual principle: they were formed
by force, and by force they were broken. Thus it was generally the first business of the royal successor to subdue the
insurgent princes and rebellious peoples and set the yoke of
empire again upon their necks. Law and order had to be
re-established. Such procedure was common enough in the
history of Egypt and Babylon, but Israel was not at any
time a world empire. The scene portrayed here is overdrawn.
The kings and princes of earth were never subject to Israel,
and even in her greatest days no such claim could be made.
Scholars have pointed to the times of David, Solomon, Jo-
siah, Uzziah, Hezekiah, Aristobulus I, and Alexander Jan-
naeus, but there is no satisfaction to be obtained from any
of these identifications. Such terms as are used here were in
place with reference to Egypt or Babylon or Assyria, but
they are wholly out of place with reference to Israel at any
period of her history. The poet here is "drawing the long
bow" and giving rein to fancy, and why not? For it was a
high day in the national life, and the Hebrew was not accustomed to speak of such events in common terms. This is *the
original reference of the psalm.*

ii

Nothing is lost by this interpretation. Rather the gain is
ours. For we need not stop with the original reference, but,
beginning there, we go on to see how the wider reference,
that was later given, is fully justified and sustained. It is not
without reason that from earliest times men have regarded
these psalms as Messianic in the Christian sense of that
term. What if there should be found here a difference as
well as a similarity to those alien songs? Israel may well
have expressed its own peculiar genius through a literary

form and thought-pattern that were borrowed. Just as the
Creation story was taken over from alien sources and baptized with a total immersion so that in Hebrew hands it
became "a thing of beauty and a joy for ever," so something
similar has happened here. Israel was indeed a small people
but *Israel had a great God*. The accession of an Israelite
king might seem an insignificant thing from the viewpoint
of world empires, but it signified a great deal from the viewpoint of Hebrew faith. For the king was the Messiah of
Jehovah, and Jehovah was Lord of history, Lord of the
world. All the resources of Jehovah were behind little Israel's
king, for he was the vicegerent of the Almighty. He was the
instrument of the divine purpose and that purpose concerned the world. He might prove a poor instrument, but he
was the Anointed of Jehovah, and Jehovah was neither poor
nor small. Without that significant thought this psalm
might seem only a piece of bombast on the part of the
Hebrew nation, but with that thought the psalm becomes
the expression of profound religious faith. The reference
here is not national but theocentric; behind the king the
psalmist sees God. One might say he sees the king not at
all, but only Jehovah. There is rebellion here and opposition, but it is the rebellion and opposition of a human world
against the divine ruler. It is "against Jehovah and against
his Anointed."

Thus in the second strophe (verses 4–6)—if we may use
the term strophe here—we see where the poet's thoughts are
centered. Over against, and exalted high above, the muttering, sputtering rage of the tumultuous throng of rebels he
sees Jehovah. High and lifted up, in the calm and serenity
of his own eternity, the Almighty looks down—and laughs!
This thought of "le Dieu qui rit" (the God who laughs)
may be a huge piece of anthropomorphism to us, but nothing less forceful could express the contrast which the poet
feels. "Like a cirrhus cloud on a summer day up there in the

blue sky" (Weiser), away from the fuming and the fretting of rebellious men, Jehovah sits serenely calm and undisturbed. The view from aloft gives another idea of things and affords an entirely different perspective. Seen from that lofty height men look like ants down there, and their vastest enterprises shrink to ridiculously small proportions when viewed from heaven's height. But let these men beware, for God may pass from laughter to anger, and they will feel its sore brunt. For Jehovah has set his king in Zion, and to rebel against his Anointed is to rebel against God. Verse 6 should probably be read as the Greek version reads it:

> For I have been set as king by him
> On Zion, his holy hill.

Here we come face to face with "the divine right of kings." This man is called of God to be his representative. God will own him for a son. "The Lord is king," but his kingship is administered by human representatives. There may be here traces of ideas common to the whole Orient. But again we should mark the differences, for it is the difference that is noteworthy. The king in Egypt was the son of the god by physical generation, and thus most peoples thought of their kings. But here, in verse 7, the formula used is that of adoption, and that signifies here that *the status is not conferred by nature but by divine decree* on the occasion of the king's accession to the throne. With the conferring of the status of sonship goes the assignment of the inheritance. The king is invested with all the rights and privileges of his office and summoned to discharge his lofty task (verses 8, 9). This is expressed in phrases that could find no point of contact in Israel's history. It may be added, also, that these expressions are far removed from our thought of him of whom it is written:

> A bruised reed he shall not break
> And smoking flax he will not quench.
>
> (ISAIAH 42:3)

The Jew, under long oppression, did come at times by a delirium of conscience that was born of a famine of justice, and was apt to see and speak words flaming red. But we need not be slow to say that this expression of the psalmist is sub-Christian. He had not the full light of the larger dispensation. Setting that aside, however, we can say that such language would be relevant in the mouth of the Babylonian or Assyrian king but it is irrelevant with reference to Israel's history. The words are out of place if we think of historical situations. But they are assuredly *not out of place if we think of vital faith and religious values.* It is this latter aspect that makes them utterly real and relevant, for it is the voice of prophetic faith that dares to hope and knows that its hope and confidence will be vindicated. It is this that differentiates the psalm from every Egyptian or Babylonian parallel and makes Hebrew psalmody unique and singular. The king has the earth for his inheritance because Jehovah is his God, because the earth is Jehovah's and the king is his son.

iii

Thus the last strophe (10–12) turns back on the first. It is an admonition to the rebels to bethink themselves of what they are attempting; their defiance is against Almighty God. Verse 11 is difficult in its present form and it would seem that there has been a dislocation of the text. The Hebrew metrical form requires that the words "kiss the Son" should end the second line of verse 11 rather than begin the twelfth verse. Moreover, the word used for "son" is the Aramaic form *bar,* whereas in verse 7 the word used for son is the proper Hebrew word *ben.* It is highly improbable that the poet would use two different words for son in the same poem. In addition to this the expression "rejoice with trembling" represents a combination of Hebrew words found nowhere else, and it represents a mental emotion and spiritual commotion impossible to a Hebrew. For these reasons it seems desirable to adopt the suggestion given in Kittel's critical edition of the Hebrew text and to read:

> Serve the Lord (Jehovah) with fear
> And tremblingly kiss his feet.

This entails only a rearrangement of the consonants in the text and it accords with the fundamental law of parallelism in the verse structure. It agrees, too, with all we know from the monuments which show subject peoples prostrating themselves before their conqueror. In these ancient pictures we can see those tyrants sitting on their thrones with their feet resting on the necks of subjugated rebels. The psalm then concludes by turning from the negative side to the positive and ends with a rhapsody of joy over rebellion ended and order restored.

Happy they who take refuge in him!

iv

Thus we see the earthly king receding into the background and God himself filling the foreground. In that sense we may still interpret the psalm with Messianic reference. In that sense it speaks not only to its own time but to all time. It opens with a situation that was frequent and local, but it widens out to endless prospects. It concludes, therefore, with a note that is universal and unique. Thus the New Testament writers are justified when they lift it out of its transient setting and interpret it with reference to the eternal counsels of God (Acts 13:33, Hebrews 1:5; 5:5). It may be true that they did not recognise "the pit from which it was digged and the rock from which it was hewn," but they shared the lofty faith that inspired it and they made that faith explicit by their interpretation.

10

A LAMENT OF THE INDIVIDUAL

PSALM 51

THE HEART MAKES THE THEOLOGIAN

1   Have mercy upon me, O God, according to thy loving-
kindness:
according to the multitude of thy tender mercies blot
out my transgressions.

2   Wash me thoroughly from mine iniquity,
and cleanse me from my sin.

3   For I acknowledge my transgressions,
and my sin is ever before me.

4   Against thee, thee only, have I sinned,
and done this evil in thy sight;
that thou mightest be justified when thou speakest,
and be clear when thou judgest.

5   Behold I was shapen in iniquity,
and in sin did my mother conceive me.

6 Behold, thou desirest truth in the inward parts;
and in the hidden *part* thou shalt make me to know
wisdom.

7 Purge me with hyssop, and I shall be clean;
wash me, and I shall be whiter than snow.

8 Make me to hear joy and gladness,
that the bones *which* thou hast broken may rejoice.

9 Hide thy face from my sins,
and blot out all mine iniquities.

10 Create in me a clean heart, O God,
and renew a right spirit within me.

11 Cast me not away from thy presence;
and take not thy Holy Spirit from me.

12 Restore unto me the joy of thy salvation,
and uphold me with *thy free* spirit.

13 Then will I teach transgressors thy ways,
and sinners shall be converted unto thee.

14 Deliver me from blood-guiltiness, O God,
and my tongue shall sing aloud of thy righteousness.

15 O Lord, open thou my lips:
and my mouth shall show forth thy praise.

16 For thou desirest not sacrifice, else would I give *it,*
thou delightest not in burnt offering.

17 The sacrifices of God are a broken spirit:
a broken and a contrite heart, O God, thou wilt not
despise.

18 Do good in thy good pleasure unto Zion:
build thou the walls of Jerusalem.

19 Then shalt thou be pleased with the sacrifices of
righteousness,
with burnt offering and whole burnt offering:
then shall they offer bullocks upon thine altar.

This song is the fourth in the group known as the *Penitential Psalms* and it will serve also as illustration of the *Individual Lament*. By reason of its profound spiritual intensity and insight it is one of the most loved songs. Here we stand in the forecourt of the Christian temple, as, in most impressive fashion, the great realities of Sin, Grace, and Forgiveness are set forth. These are the great thoughts which fill the mind of the singer and he deals with them on the basis of experience. Here we have an analysis of sin which rivals that given by Saint Paul in his Epistle to the Romans, and it exceeds anything else in the Old Testament by its spiritual vision and its perception of moral realities. Here we have the spiritual earnestness of Saint Paul and the ethical and religious genius of Saint John. By its sheer inwardness and penetrating spiritual analysis it has laid hold on all the generations and has become one of the most precious jewels in the "treasury of David." The superscription would assign it to David, "when he went in to Bathsheba," but such a superscription has no historical value and may be set aside. Apart from the fact that there is nothing in the psalm itself to warrant such a superscription, and that what is said in the psalm seems wholly inconsistent with what is recorded of David and that sordid incident in his career, the lofty ideas of spiritual religion herein expressed could not have been thought of in that early period. Verse 18 makes it clear that the date of the psalm cannot be earlier than the Exile when the walls of Jerusalem were laid low. The writer is plainly one who has drunk deep at the fountain of prophetic doctrine and felt the liberating influence of the truths which those spokesmen of God proclaimed. The song needs no signature for it speaks from life to life and deals with fundamental matters in a high spirit of seriousness.

i

In conformity with the usual form of such *Laments* the singer begins with a loud cry to God, and this cry is not, as is usual in such songs, a cry for relief from physical suffering but for forgiveness. Some commentators are of opinion that there is no reference to sickness or suffering but this seems unlikely in view of verses 8, 14.

There is no regular strophic structure in this song, for, as in the books of Hosea and Job, the atmosphere is too tense and the spiritual conflict is too great to endure an ordered symmetrical form. But there is a close sequence of thought which we should not fail to observe. The opening cry (1–3) is followed by the confession and recognition of the "exceeding sinfulness of sin" (4–6); then comes the prayer for remission of sin (7–9), a plea for inward renewal (10–13), ending with a vow of thanksgiving. Verses 18, 19 are a later addition added by some prosaic soul for whom the singer's flight was much too daring.

The brief opening cry sets forth with poignancy the theme. We may set it in something like its original form and translate thus:

191383

> Have mercy on me, O God, according to thy love,
>> In thy vast compassions wash my sins away.
> Wash me clean from my iniquity,
>> And from my transgression purify thou me.

Here we have a conscience oppressed by its load of guilt and the knowledge that only God's love (*Chesed*) will avail to put things right. There is no protestation of innocence as often meets us in the Psalter (Psalm 44), nor any thought of countervailing service for man and God, no thought at all of any works by which he might eke out the grace of God. "Nothing in my hand I bring." It is the devout attitude of one whose only hope is in the mercy and compassion (*rachamim*) of God. This alone can "blot out" the record from God's book and cleanse his "o'ercharged bosom of this perilous stuff." "Not all the blood of beasts on Jewish altars slain" can bring peace to his troubled spirit. Only God can do that, and to God he cries. The writer is in no doubt here. He knows his sin: it thrusts its hateful presence upon him. But not only does he know the fact of his sin: he knows its nature. Here the singer probes deeply and speaks a great word about the tragic reality. For sin is *sin against God*. All sin, no matter against whom it is committed, is ultimately that which "is evil in thy sight." Kittel, Staerk, and Weiser maintain this is what the writer means, but it seems preferable to adopt another interpretation, for which we may claim the support of Gunkel. Without diminishing in the least the spiritual nature of this Old Testament saint we would rather think that here he claims to be free of offences against his fellow-men. He has not defrauded widows nor removed landmarks nor oppressed the poor—all these offences were charged against Job by his friends (Job 22:5f.) —nor has he been guilty of anti-social conduct. Rather his sins are the sins of the saint who must always be most conscious of his shortcomings. No one is more conscious of these than the Apostle Paul himself. The lofty souls who have the clearest vision of God have always the deepest and most agonising consciousness of sin. The matter lies wholly between the soul and God, and between no others.

In verses 3, 4 the reference is to his suffering which the singer admits is deserved and merited. It is the reaction of the divine holiness against human sin, and therein the divine righteousness is revealed. In his own heart the poet knows his sin, and by his confession God's honor is vindicated. The current theology is upheld here in a way that would have delighted the friends of Job.

The interpretation of Kittel, Staerk, and Weiser would

set this psalm on a still higher level. For those scholars assert that the psalmist here is giving expression to a Pauline thought such as is expressed in Romans 11:32, where the Apostle, wrestling with the problem of sin, concludes:

> For God hath shut up all unto disobedience that he might have mercy upon all.
> O the depths of the riches both of the wisdom and the knowledge of God! How unsearchable are his judgments, and his ways past finding out! . . .
> For of him and through him and unto him are all things. To him be the glory for ever. Amen.

Man's sin finally redounds to the glory of God, and in the midst of the divine judgment on sin is revealed the love that lifts sin away and renews human life. In one glance the Apostle beholds judgment and mercy, and mercy triumphs over judgment. It may be possible that the poet had this wondrous insight, but the present writer feels on safer ground with the interpretation he has offered in the foregoing.

But further still will the singer travel with the burden that weighs upon his soul. With Pauline insistency and urgency he will track it down to its last lair that he may deal with it adequately and finally (verse 5). This is not to be taken as a palliation of his sin, as if a man should lay the blame on environment and heredity. The poet is too profoundly earnest on the moral side to seek refuge in the physical: he is concerned to find out the real nature of this awful thing. This crippling and debilitating thing seems to be set in the very nature of men. It seems to be handed down through the generations by the physical act of procreation like an evil entail. There is no specific doctrine of Original Sin here—that does not emerge in the Old Testament—but only the recognition of the fact that, by his natural constitution, man is more prone to evil than to good. Paul knew that well, and so did the Roman poet Ovid. We

live in a world where it seems natural and easy to go against
the will of God. The good that we would, we do not, and
the evil that we would not, that we do. We are "beset by the
hateful siege of contraries": we approve the better but follow the worse. It is not a question of individual transgressions, but of the whole set and drift of human life. The will
of man is set against God and spiritual excellence cannot
evolve on such a basis but must be created from without.
There is certainly no thought of belittling the marriage
bond, as that thought emerges in monasticism (verse 5).
Still less is there any suggestion that his birth was outside
the bonds of wedlock. The poet is going down to the roots of
things and finds himself caught in a vice from which he
cannot free himself. The corruption is deep-seated in human
nature and something radical is required. The spiritual must
invade the natural with overwhelming power to renew if
man is to become what God intended him to be. The poet
sets this forth as something which he has discovered by
divine inspiration, and from his emphasis one might infer
that a doctrine of the heritage of sin was somewhat novel at
that period. Verse 6 is difficult but the general sense is clear:

> Lo, thou desirest truth in the inward parts,
> and thou teachest me wisdom in my inmost being.

This must refer to what has gone before and it would seem
that the singer ascribes the inspiration of his confession and
his insight into the real nature of sin to the prevenient grace
of God. He is able to say what he does say because God has
enabled him to see right to the roots and realities of the
matter.

ii

Now comes the prayer for forgiveness. The first phrase is
taken from the cult and refers to the ritual for cleansing in
the case of leprosy (Leviticus 14:4f.) or to the case of one
who has been in contact with a corpse (Numbers 19:18).

The words are used here without any such thought and "whiter than snow" may be derived from Isaiah 1:18 though such a thought was common enough. In verse 8 it is better to read (with the Syriac version):

Satisfy me with joy and gladness
that the bones which thou hast broken may rejoice.

There may be no reference to bodily sickness in these words —as both Kittel and Weiser think—but it seems better to believe such is implied. While, indeed, the whole thought of physical sickness recedes into the background and the main emphasis is on the weight of guilt that burdens the conscience, the thought of pressing pain does emerge in both verse 8 and verse 14. The removal of this stroke would give the assurance that God was dealing graciously with his sin and the natural would thus become the vehicle of the spiritual. Sin must first be lifted away and the former joy of uninterrupted communion with God restored. Forgiveness and removal of sin are not enough. Justification must be followed by sanctification. Because of the inherent incapacity of human nature to walk before God with a perfect heart, the psalmist now widens his prayer to a petition for newness of life, and the word he uses in verse 10 for "create" is the word used in Genesis 1:1 of God's creative activity. That word is not used of human action but only of God's creative action. God's creative power must be put forth once again in the mercy of retrieval and redemption, and it is put forth to fashion what Paul calls "a new creation." Jeremiah had dreamed of this in his thought of the New Covenant (Jeremiah 31:31f.), and the same thought finds repeated expression in Ezekiel (11:17f.; 36:25f.). Here we see the Old Testament roots of a thought that finds varied expression in the New Testament:

But after that the kindness and love of God toward man appeared, not by works of righteousness which we have done, but according to his mercy he saved

> us by the washing of regeneration and renewing of
> the Holy Ghost, which is shed on us abundantly
> through Jesus Christ our Savior; that being justi-
> fied by his grace we should be made heirs according
> to the hope of eternal life.   (TITUS 3:4f.)

God's creative power is put forth once again to renew his
child: the divine miracle of creation is repeated in the
singer's experience. The new life can be lived only by men
freed from the downdrag of the past and empowered with a
divine energy that keeps life in the highways of God (verse
10). Great prayers are always as simple as this: they fly
straight up and bring the blessing down. The spirit that
aforetime moved so uncertainly amid the seductions and
temptations of life is now replaced by a spirit of steadfast-
ness that knows no trembling or indecision. He is struggling
here to express what Paul means by "Christ in us": it is
such close communion that he seeks (verses 11, 12). To have
unbroken communion with God in the uninterrupted sunshine of his grace—that is the height of his prayer. Here the
poet says something new and unprecedented, for here we
have reference to the Holy Spirit. Only in one other passage
is the expression used (Isaiah 63:10), and there it has not
as full meaning as here. The closest parallel to this unique
expression is in the last of the Penitential Psalms:

> Let thy good spirit lead me in a right way.
>   (PSALM 143:10)

The thought of the spirit of God was not foreign to the Old
Testament but it was generally thought of in the way of
physical energy. There was something *demonic* in it, one
might say, as it "rushed upon" Samson or Saul and made
them mighty to conquer. Elsewhere it is conceived of in a
less boisterous fashion: it rests upon the wise as a spirit of
wisdom, upon the Messiah as a spirit of insight and understanding (Isaiah 9:3), but here it rises to the highest level
and is regarded as pure moral energy. It is a good spirit

because it is God's spirit, and it is a holy spirit because it
partakes of his essence. Its possession is the sign and seal of
our redemption and through it life is lifted "into the heavenly places" and obedience becomes second nature. It is a
spirit of obedience because it is the moving impulse of a life
that is in tune with the infinite. And forasmuch as this man
knows that God's gifts are not to have and to hold but that
he is saved to serve, he will not stay nor tarry but, under the
driving of the spirit, he will go forth to tell what wondrous
things for him the Lord hath wrought (verse 13). That is
the expression of his gratitude and faith. Men who have
shared this experience know its compelling power, and this
compulsion testifies to its genuineness.

> We cannot but speak the things which we saw and
> heard.   (ACTS 4:20)

iii

Now comes the conclusion in the form of a vow. This is
common procedure in such *Laments of the Individual*. The
singer usually promises to offer a sacrifice as a token of his
thanksgiving for the marvelous boon bestowed on him by
divine grace.

The literal rendering of verse 14 is "deliver me from
bloods," for which the English version gives "deliver me
from blood-guiltiness." The reference here cannot be to any
evil deed which the poet had committed: such a thought
seems impossible in the light of what has preceded here. It
must, therefore, refer to some untoward calamity that
threatened to fall upon this man at the hand of his fellows.
Kittel thinks the singer was risking his life by preaching the
gospel of redeeming grace, for men had known him as a
thorough-going bad man and would not credit his conversion. Just as Paul had to be safeguarded from the fury of
distrustful Christians who had only known him as "breath-
ing out threatenings and slaughter" against the infant

church, so was it with this psalmist. Gunkel rightly rejects this interpretation, for it was inconceivable that the psalm could be written by such a character. It seems wiser to read for the Hebrew word *damim* (bloods) the word *dumah* (silence). This word, by an extension of its original meaning, came to mean *land of silence,* and was, therefore, equivalent to *death.* This seems very probable, for the psalmist, having experienced the signal redemption and renewing power of God, prays that he may be given the opportunity to proclaim and publish what God has done. It is the expression of joy in, and eagerness for, the service of God. The door of opportunity has opened and he prays God that he may enter in abundantly to find increasing joy and to yield unceasing praise to his Redeemer. As the poet proceeds we see that he has absorbed the lofty doctrine of the great prophets and is passing by them all to stand beside the New Testament writer who tells us:

> The hour cometh, and now is, when the true worshippers shall worship the Father in spirit and in truth; for the Father seeketh such to worship him.
> God is a spirit: and they that worship him must worship *him* in spirit and in truth.
>
> (JOHN 4:23, 24)

The words of Amos and Isaiah, of Hosea and Jeremiah, had here fallen on fruitful soil. Here is one who had learned that "to obey is better than sacrifice" and who comes before God with no material sacrifice but only with a humble spirit and a contrite heart. Again we follow the Syriac and read:

> For thou takest no pleasure in sacrifice:
> In proffered burnt-offering thou hast no delight.
> The sacrifices of God are a broken spirit—
> and a contrite heart, O God, thou wilt not despise.
>
> (VERSES 16, 17)

The words which the psalmist uses here are big words whose meaning men could not grasp in that day and age. Here are

seminal thoughts that could ripen only under the light of
the Christian Gospel. What God requires is not the blood
of beasts nor altars smoking with sacrifice but a heart that
renounces all claims upon God and humbles itself to the
dust in the knowledge that God alone can do for men what
they can never do for themselves, a heart awed by his judgments and subdued by the revelation of his grace. That is
the abiding attitude of the life of faith. Religion here ceases
to be occupied with externals: it becomes rooted and
grounded in the inmost heart, and life is hid in God.

iv

The last two verses have been added by a later writer.
Here is the witness of the greatness of the poet's insight.
For lesser men could never climb such heights of spiritual
vision. For most men the ethic of the thing done takes the
place of the ethic of the clean heart. Daring thoughts like
those expressed in this poem could not be left at large in the
world; the time was not yet. And so a later prosaic spirit
sought to mold them to the conventional pattern (*verses* 18,
19). Obviously this writer was living at a later time when
the religious cult had been disrupted and the walls of Jerusalem were laid low. He seeks to justify the opinion on sacrifice which our poet had expressed, but only as motivated
by a temporary necessity. When Jerusalem is restored the
cult will function once more, and altars will reek with the
blood of bulls and goats. We may be thankful for this epilogue, for it may be that through its presence here the psalm
was preserved to us. Without it the lofty ideas of the original singer might have passed into the limbo of forgotten
things. The writer of the epilogue built better than he knew,
for by this anti-climax he preserved this precious jewel for
all generations. Compared to the psalm itself the epilogue is
"as moonlight unto sunlight and as water unto wine."

11

A PSALM OF TRUST

PSALM 23

THE LORD IS MY SHEPHERD

1 The Lord is my shepherd; I shall not want.

2 He maketh me to lie down in green pastures:
he leadeth me beside the still waters.

3 He restoreth my soul:
he leadeth me in the paths of righteousness for his
name's sake.

4 Yea, though I walk through the valley of the shadow
of death,
I will fear no evil: for thou art with me;
thy rod and thy staff they comfort me.

5 Thou preparest a table before me in the presence of mine
enemies:
thou anointest my head with oil: my cup runneth over.

6 Surely goodness and mercy shall follow me all the days
of my life:
and I will dwell in the house of the Lord for ever.

This psalm is the pearl and crown of all the *Praises of Israel*. Its simple beauty has touched the hearts of all mankind, and from the womb to the tomb it has proved itself the stay and comfort of all God's children. It formed the first fond prayer we learned at a mother's knee, and with its words upon their lips brave men have breathed their last. It is the crystallisation of piety through two thousand years and more, the concentrated devotion of all the generations. We turn to it for comfort and release as we turn to the matchless story of *the Prodigal Son* in the New Testament. Theology we may not understand but we need religion, and religion is here in its simplest form. It finds us in the deepest parts of our being: it grips us and holds us as nothing else can. The creed is rarely recited in the Church of Scotland, and if a man were asked to state his creed he would most probably put it in the words of this psalm and recite the words he had learned at his mother's knee.

> The Lord's my shepherd, I'll not want.
> He makes me down to lie,
> In pastures green: he leadeth me
> The quiet waters by.
> My soul he doth restore again;
> And me to walk doth make
> Within the paths of righteousness,
> Ev'n for his own name's sake.
> Yea, though I walk in death's dark vale,
> Yet will I fear none ill;
> For thou art with me; and thy rod
> And staff me comfort still.
> My table thou hast furnished
> In presence of my foes;
> My head thou dost with oil anoint,
> And my cup overflows.
> Goodness and mercy all my life
> Shall surely follow me:
> And in God's house for evermore
> My dwelling-place shall be.

A creed in this form has the merit of simplicity and is easily remembered. It holds, too, a depth and weight of theology which we may try to fathom. For there is more here than appears on the surface. To analyse this song may seem like attempting to "paint the lily and gild refined gold," for in the process of distillation the essential spirit may elude us and be lost for ever. It has to be admitted that in the matter of interpretation such a fate has, all too often, befallen this lovely gem of the Psalter.

i

A main difficulty of interpretation lies in the apparent fact that the psalm does not present a unified viewpoint. It would seem as if in verse 5 the imagery changes from a pastoral scene to that of an indoor banquet and the temple at Jerusalem (the house of the Lord). But that break is only apparent and there is no real discontinuity in the psalm. It is a unity throughout, and this will become obvious as we proceed to examine the figures used. Kittel in his commentary gives as title for the psalm *Yahwe mein Hirt und mein Wirt* (Yahwe my shepherd and my host), and it is unfortunate that we cannot reproduce this play of words in the English. But with this title in our mind we may proceed to an examination of the contents, and observe how the unified viewpoint is won.

The psalm opens with the pastoral scene and though it requires seven words in English to render this it is to be noted there are only four words in the Hebrew, and those words are full of music. They fall like a benediction on the ear:

Yahwe ro-i lo echsar

That is not how we would naturally express the thought of the Psalmist. We would deduce the second clause from the

first and insert the word *therefore* to show that the second is
the natural and logical conclusion of the opening statement.
But Hebrew thought was not philosophical and he did not
think with our thought processes. Hebrew thought was intuitive and immediate, and those two radiant certainties visited his soul simultaneously and at the same moment. That
is not how we think, but it is how the Hebrew thought.
Here, too, we see more of Hebrew thought, for the Old Testament thinks first of the group and only secondarily of the
individual. The faith of the individual has been kindled at
the community altar, for it must be noted that the term
"shepherd" is a term denoting relation to a group. Israel
often thought of her God in this manner:

> Give ear, O Shepherd of Israel,
> thou that leadest Jacob like a flock:
> thou that dwellest *between* the cherubim,
> shine forth. (PSALM 80:1)

Isaiah of the Exile loves this thought and uses it frequently
(Isaiah 40:11; 49:9f; 63:14) as does also Ezekiel (34:10).
The thought of God's watchful superintending providence
cannot be better expressed. But here the singer is individu-
alising the thought and gives us this *Psalm of Trust* (*cp.*
Psalm 11). The singer may have been an old man full of
days who has "seen God's hand through a lifetime, and all
was for best."

The business of the shepherd is to know the good grazing
grounds where the green lush grass is found, and the water-
ing-places which might frequently be at some distance from
the pasture-lands. To these the shepherd leads the sheep,
for of themselves they know not the way. The way to the
grass-lands might be long, for changing pastures must be
sought from time to time. When the sheep have eaten their
fill, he leads them to the watering-place, and there the tired
sheep rest beside "the waters of rest." The word used for

rest, *menucha,* was often used by the Jews to describe the land of Palestine, the promised land, to which they came after all their weary wanderings in the wilderness. All this is in the singer's mind as he thinks of the tender care and provision that brings back strength to the tired sheep. The word used for soul in verse 3 (*nephesh*) means nothing more than the physical life. Indeed a good translation would be "he revives me," and D. B. MacDonald [1] renders the verse, "my appetite he keeps restoring." Nor is it necessary to read any profound theological meaning into the phrase *paths of righteousness.* The writer means no more than right paths, paths that are really paths. There were so many tracks that led only to the edge of the ravine, and silly sheep would wander in those tracks that were not right paths, but the shepherd knows the paths that arrive, that get somewhere and lead to a satisfying goal. The shepherd leads the sheep in such right paths because he is a good shepherd and desires to be known as such. He has a reputation to maintain and he will not let his good name be lost. He does what he does *for his name's sake.* There are hirelings whose only thought is of money and they think not of their duty as shepherds; they have no proper care of the sheep. But the good shepherd finds his chiefest joy in the maintenance of his good name: none will point the finger of scorn at him or say he was false to the highest standards of the pastoral office. His glory he will not give to another, nor will he suffer his fair fame to be blasphemed. He will fulfill all that his good name demands.

The sheep, too, may wander to the deep dark shadowed places where in the shadows the wild beasts lurk, or it may be wilder men. For in Palestine the sun shines with such brilliance and the shadows cast are so deep and dark in the natural depressions of the land that beasts of prey can lurk

[1] *The Hebrew Literary Genius,* p. 51.

there in safety and pounce at will upon the unsuspecting silly sheep. David knew this well and he proved himself a good shepherd by slaying a lion and a bear that set upon his flock (I Samuel 17:34f.). The good shepherd is willing to risk his life for his sheep. For that reason the shepherd carried not only the staff or familiar shepherd's crook, but also a club studded with nails to brain those wild beasts or beat down robber men. The modern shepherd in the East carries his shepherd's crook and a gun, the crook for the care of the sheep and the gun for the flock's defence. Some scholars would change the word *they comfort me* (*verse* 4) and read instead *they lead me,* but the word should be retained for its wealth of meaning. It signifies "to help another, choked with grief or fear, to breathe freely and give his heart air." [2] In the *deep darkness,* which is a better rendering than *the valley of the shadow of death,* there is nothing a man needs more than comfort of this remedial kind.

ii

Here, however, the pastoral scene seems to change and give place to another centered in a banqueting house. But as George Adam Smith has pointed out in his beautiful study of this psalm it is still the pastoral scene that occupies the singer. For here we have to do with the desert law of hospitality, which together with the law of blood revenge constitutes the fundamental background of nomad life. It may well be that both those desert laws are reflected here, for the singer is thinking of something he has seen in the desert when on a day he saw the fugitive from blood vengeance fleeing across the desert with the avengers on his trail. In front of the fugitive lies the shepherd's tent and toward it he speeds with all his flagging energy. If he may but touch the ropes of that tent or throw himself within the entrance,

[3] *The Song of Our Syrian Guest* (The Pilgrim Press, Boston), pp. 18–20.

he will be safe from those avengers. He who sheds man's blood, by man shall his blood be shed. So runs the desert law but across that fierce law cuts the other humaner law of desert hospitality. Within that little tent the man will be safe, safe as the rock of Gibraltar—even safer. The shepherd will receive him and entertain with the best available, anointing his guest's head with oil and setting forth his best provision. Though it were his own brother—such cases are on record—that had been slain, the shepherd will not violate that law of hospitality. Outside the tent the avengers grim stand lowering and scowling, but the fugitive is safe from all their fury. He can sit there at ease and enjoy the shepherd's hospitality to the full. *But only for a time.* There is a limit to this hospitality, a time limit of two days and the intervening night, only "so long as the food is in his bowels." When that period expires his immunity ceases and he must go forth and bide his bloody assize. And as the writer thinks of that he thinks also of the divine hospitality which knows no limit but abides for ever (verse 6).

For length of days is what the Psalmist says of his abiding: he could not say more. Immortality was not yet brought to light. It is the Gospel alone that enables us to say *for ever.*

Thus the psalm that opened with pastoral beauty lingers in it right to the end.

Alternative Interpretation

Another interpretation that likewise treats the psalm as a unity is given by W. A. Knight [3] in his little brochure entitled *The Song of Our Syrian Guest.* The writer there refers to *verse 5* as indicating an ancient Eastern custom called "the rodding of the sheep." It will be best to give the writer's own words here.

[3] *The Song of Our Syrian Guest,* (The Pilgrim Press, Boston) pp. 18–20.

The psalm has sung of the whole round of the day's wanderings, all the needs of the sheep, all the care of the shepherd. Now the psalm closes with the last scene of the day. At the door of the sheepfold the shepherd stands, and the rodding of the sheep takes place. The shepherd stands, turning his body to let the sheep pass: he is the door, as Christ said of himself. With his rod he holds back the sheep while he inspects them one by one as they pass into the fold. He has the horn filled with olive oil, and he has cedar-tar, and he anoints a knee bruised on the rocks or a side scratched by thorns. And here comes one that is not bruised but is simply worn and exhausted; he bathes its face and head with refreshing olive oil, and he takes the large two-handled cup, and dips it brimming full with water from the vessel provided for the purpose, and he lets the weary sheep drink. There is nothing finer in the psalm than this. God's care is not for the wounded only but for the worn and weary also. *He anointeth my head with oil, my cup runneth over.*

And then when the day is gone, and the sheep are snug within the fold, what contentment, what rest under the starry sky! Then comes the thought of deepest repose and comfort; *surely goodness and mercy shall follow me all the days of my life,* as they have followed me through all the wanderings of the day now ended.

The song dies away as the heart that God has watched and tended breathes this grateful vow before the roaming of the day is forgotten in sleep. *I will—not shall, but will*—for it is decision, a settled purpose, a holy vow: I will dwell in the house of the Lord for ever. And the song ends and the sheep are at rest, safe in the Good Shepherd's fold.

12

A PSALM DEALING WITH THE LAW

PSALM 15

THE GENTLEMAN'S PSALM

1 Lord, who shall abide in thy tabernacle?
  who shall dwell in thy holy hill?

2 He that walketh uprightly, and worketh righteousness,
  and speaketh the truth in his heart.

3 *He that* backbiteth not with his tongue,
  nor doeth evil to his neighbour,
  nor taketh up a reproach against his neighbour.

4 In whose eyes a vile person is contemned;
  but he honoureth them that fear the Lord.
  He that sweareth to his own hurt, and changeth not.

5 *He that* putteth not out his money to usury,
  nor taketh reward against the innocent.
  He that doeth these things shall never be moved.

The question as to the quality of church membership
must always engage the attention of church leaders. It is the
question that constantly engaged the attention of those

responsible for the moral and spiritual welfare of ancient
Israel. Even then men observed that Israel according to the
flesh was not identical with Israel according to the spirit,
and they perceived that certain moral demands must be
made of a people whose God was the Lord. The requirements of that ancient church are here set forth in the form
of question and answer. The question is asked by an individual who may be speaking on behalf of a group, and the
answer is given by one who seems to be responsible for all
things being "done decently and in order" in the realm of
public worship. In the present instance this answering official is "the guardian of the threshold," whose function in
ancient temples was to exclude any who were unfit or unworthy to enter. We might say of this psalm that it lays
down the conditions of church membership; it may thus be
regarded as a manual for catechumens, such as was used in
the early church and is commonly employed at the present
time. From this viewpoint it is not difficult to understand
why it has been called "the Gentleman's Psalm." Perhaps
we should say Christian gentleman, for some terms of nobil-
ity have lost their original significance and fallen into
disrepute.

Gunkel classifies this psalm as a *Tora liturgy*, that is a
liturgy dealing with the Law or instruction. The term *instruction* is better here, for it refers to that general direction
and spiritual guidance which the priest was accustomed to
offer to his people in all ways and walks of life. Similar litur-
gies occur in Isaiah 33:14–16 and Micah 6:6–8 and also in
Psalm 24:3ff. These psalms are liturgical in the sense that
two or more parties take part in them.

i

The three notes of the true church, according to the
Protestant Reformers are a) preaching the Gospel, b) the

administration of the sacraments, c) the maintenance of discipline. The first two notes require no particular explanation and are easily enough understood. But the third note requires emphasis, for the failure of the church today is largely due to its failure to maintain discipline in the ranks of its members. One has but to read the epistles of Paul to understand what is wanted here. Paul knew how to preach the Gospel, and from him, too, we have the words of the institution of the Lord's Supper (I Corinthians 11:23ff.). But Paul knew well that something more is required. The churches had to be maintained at a Christian standard of character, and to that end Paul preached a strong Christian ethic. He not only preached that ethic, but applied it to the life and activity of those churches. He told people not only what they ought to do, but also what they dare not do if they intended to remain Christians.

> But fornication, and all uncleanness, or covetousness, let it not even be named among you, as becometh saints; nor filthiness, nor foolish talking, or jesting, which are not befitting: but rather giving of thanks.   (EPHESIANS 5:3, 4)

There were occasions in the Apostle's life when he had to intervene forcibly and expel people from the church, which was the fellowship of believers. That is the maintenance of discipline, the keeping of church members at a Christian level of character. The New Testament church can be maintained on a Christian level only as its members reveal a Christian standard of character, only as they accept life as the high calling of God in Christ. The church might well reduce its membership in quantity and thereby increase its quality, for members who are spiritually strong will achieve more than our present indisciplined hordes. It may well be that a *minister's success should be judged by his power to empty a church,* for that could signify that the Christian claim was being presented with such force that all faint-hearted people were turning from it. With a band of selected Gideons (Judges 7:4ff.) the minister might achieve something worthwhile. In any case there is ample food for thought here.

The ancients were wiser than we are in this matter. The doors of the church were guarded precisely as the Church of Scotland used to "fence the table of the Lord." This custom still persists there in some of the smaller communions, and men are forced to "examine themselves" before they draw near to the body and blood of our Lord. This practice is ancient and well-attested and, though objections can be raised against the custom, it has elements of great value, which should not be overlooked. In those ancient temples the question was put by "the guardian of the threshold," and intending entrants to the sanctuary had to answer satisfactorily or be refused admission. "Have you observed all the ritual?" "Are you clean?" "Have you spoken the truth, and have you walked in the right way?"—these and similar questions were put to intending worshipers. Men were deterred from a rash entry into the Holy of Holies. This custom is found in Babylon, Egypt, and Greece, and it is found in the Old Testament. Those ancient cults were guarded jealously. Admonitions were inscribed upon the doors to guard against any profanation by unworthy people. Such an inscription on the door of the temple of Aesculapius at Epidauros read:

Only the pure may cross the temple threshold:
Only he is pure whose thoughts are holy.

Something similar was found on Herod's temple, where the inscription reads:

No heathen may enter the enclosure around the temple. Whosoever is caught so doing will bear the responsibility, for death is the penalty therefor.

That is in line with the primitive urge for cultic purity, and the same thing meets us in the Apocalypse of John:

> And there shall in no wise enter in anything unclean, or he that maketh an abomination and a lie: but only they that are written in the Lamb's book of life. (REVELATION 21:27)

ii

Such, then, is the general background of the psalm. The question here may be put by an individual on his own behalf, or, more probably, it is put by one who is leading a band of pilgrims who have come up out of the Dispersion to observe the feast in the temple at Jerusalem. He wishes to know the requirements that he and his group may enter in a right state. God is great and none may come into his presence save in the right and proper manner. The man desires to be the guest of God and they desire to know what the divine host requires of his guests (verse 1). That is their question and it is the business of the official to instruct them on this point. It may be worthwhile here to look at the similar passage in Micah, which shows the same procedure.

> Wherewithal shall I come before Jehovah and bow myself before the high God? Shall I come before him with burnt-offerings, with calves a year old? Will Jehovah be pleased with thousands of rams, or with ten thousands of rivers of oil? Shall I give my first-born for my transgression, the fruit of my body for the sin of my soul? He hath showed thee, O man, what is good: and what doth Jehovah require of thee, but to do justly, and to love kindness, and to walk humbly with thy God?
> (MICAH 6:6–8)

Here the perplexed worshiper is putting the question and surveying alternatives. Here, too, the priest gives definite instruction on the matter at issue. In the present psalm no alternatives are put by the questioner: a simple question is asked and a direct answer is given. The Talmud [1] remarks regarding the answer:

> David compressed the 613 commands of the Tora into 11 (Psalm 15), Isaiah into 6 (Isaiah 33:14f.), Micah into 3 (Micah 6:6–8), Amos and Habakkuk into 1 (Amos 5:4; Habakkuk 2:4).

Jesus, too, was a master of such compression (Matthew 22:37, 38), as was also Paul (Romans 1:17).

iii

Let us look at this answer which, according to the Talmud, reveals such conciseness and compression. It is certainly not the answer we would expect from a priest. There is nothing here of ritual requirements, but only a demand for ethical purity and right social attitudes. All we have read about priests and Levites in the New Testament would not lead us to expect an answer like this. There is nothing here about "tithing of mint and cummin," which seems to absorb the priests' attention in the Gospel stories. Indeed, this answer might have come from the lips of Isaiah, and we would not have thought it out of place in the Sermon on the Mount. But here it is from the lips of an Old Testament priest. It may be that we have been doing less than justice to the priests and making more than we ought of the seeming opposition of prophet and priest. This psalm certainly shows a large influence of the prophet upon the priest. In any case here the priestly official stands, and this is how he speaks. Religion to him is no external thing of rites and ceremonies: it is internalised and set within the heart of man (*verses* 2–5).

To the Hebrew religion is intensely practical. It reveals itself in character rather than in creed, in walk rather than in

---

[1] *B. Talmud, Makkoth,* 23b–24a.

talk. Truth in the heart makes a true man, and a true man
acts out the truth that is in him: he does the straight and
righteous thing. All his actions are motivated, not by external authority, but by an inward compelling passion for
truth. That issues in perfection of behavior or walk. Out of
the heart are the issues of life. Here they proceed from a
heart that is sound and true. The commands given may be
drawn from ancient forms of social life. From the stress laid
on slander and sins of the tongue we might gather that the
writer lived in a small community where gossip is apt to be
rife and often malicious.

The requirements are all grounded on the fundamental
inwardness of truth in the heart. The good man lifts no idle
tales nor does he tell lies about his neighbor. His word is as
good as his bond, and once he has given his word he will not
break it though holding to it may cost him much. He abides
by his pledged word because he is true. Righteousness, moreover, will withhold him from oppressing his fellow-man,
and he is of loftier character than to take a bribe. All this
might come from the lips of Jesus, and if there is something
in the psalm that would not have been on the lips of the
Savior we need not therefore derogate unduly from its lofty
teaching. The despising of the reprobate (verse 4) may
seem to express a sentiment less than Christian, but this
repulsion of evil is the reverse side of the writer's zeal for
truth and righteousness. He honors those who fear Jehovah,
and those who love God will hate evil. The Old Testament
produced "good haters," but though we hate evil we need
not hate the evil-doer. The Hebrew did not make that distinction, and his intense genius is frequently revealed in this
way.

> Do not I hate them, O Jehovah, that hate thee?
> And am not I grieved with those that rise up
>   against thee?

I hate them with perfect hatred:
They are become mine enemies.
                                            (PSALM 139:21, 22)

Somehow this *perfect hatred* does not seem such an un-
healthy thing, and a goodly portion of it might put blood
and iron into our modern religion which is in danger of
seeping away and evaporating into slushy sentimentality.
Doubtless the Psalmist had not yet learned to hate sin and
still love the sinner, but the Psalter is not yet the Gospel,
and the fullness of time was not yet come.

iv

The Psalter is not the Gospel, or surely this man would
have fallen on his knees and said, "Who is sufficient for
these things?" There is in the psalm a certain self-confidence which has points of contact with what we call Pharisaism. But man cannot lift himself by his own boot-straps:
salvation is of the Lord. "We are saved by grace, and that
not of ourselves: it is the gift of God" (Ephesians 2:8). That
is the word of Paul, and it is a profound word. Of this the
official may have been conscious when he spoke the final
word:

He that doeth these things shall never be moved.

Here he may be setting an ideal towards which the pilgrims
might strive. We may set beside it, as the final word of
truth, the saying of Paul, who had tried the Psalmist's way
in vain.

In him who strengthens me I am able for anything.
                          (PHILIPPIANS 4:13; Moffatt version)

13

A PSALM OF MIXED TYPE

PSALM 90

THE ETERNAL GOD

1 Lord, thou hast been our dwelling place in all generations.
2 Before the mountains were brought forth,
or ever thou hadst formed the earth and the world,
even from everlasting to everlasting thou art God.
3 Thou turnest man to destruction,
and sayest, Return, ye children of men.
4 For a thousand years in thy sight
are but as yesterday when it is past,
and *as* a watch in the night.
5 Thou carriest them away as with a flood: they are as a
sleep;
in the morning *they are* like the grass *which* groweth up.
6 In the morning it flourisheth and groweth up:
in the evening it is cut down, and withereth.
7 For we are consumed by thine anger,
and by thy wrath are we troubled.

8   Thou hast set our iniquities before thee,
      our secret *sins* in the light of thy countenance.

9   For all our days are passed away in thy wrath:
      we spend our years as a tale *that is told*.

10   The days of our years are three score years and ten;
      and if by reason of strength *they be* four score years,
      yet is their strength labour and sorrow;
      for it is soon cut off, and we fly away.

11   Who knoweth the power of thine anger?
      even according to thy fear, *so is* thy wrath.

12   So teach *us* to number our days
      that we may apply *our* hearts unto wisdom.

13   Return, O Lord, how long?
      and let it repent thee concerning thy servants.

14   O satisfy us early with thy mercy;
      that we may rejoice and be glad all our days.

15   Make us glad according to the days *wherein* thou hast
      afflicted us,
      and the years *wherein* we have seen evil.

16   Let thy work appear unto thy servants,
      and thy glory unto their children.

17   And let the beauty of the Lord our God be upon us;
      and establish thou the work of our hands upon us;
      yea, the work of our hands establish thou it.

This psalm [1] is usually associated with the most solemn moments of life, and it finds its place in the burial service of most communions. Great and lofty thoughts are here expressed, thoughts on which the human heart can stay itself in the hour of death. It opens with the fundamental

[1] According to Gunkel, *verses* 1, 2, 4 are *Hymn* type, *verses* 13–17 *Community Lament* type, while the central piece is *Individual Lament*. The present writer judges all the verses after verse 4 to be a *Community Lament*: this in the light of the Hebrew thought of Corporate Personality.

certainty of God in a world where everything seems to be in a state of flux, and the mind of man is oppressed with the sense of tears in all mortal things. The generations of men come and pass, they fall like leaves before the autumn gales, but God abides unchanging and unchanged in his mercy and protecting grace. The eternity of God alone gives meaning to the changing human scene. With large sonorous speech and lengthy lines befitting the vastness of his thought the psalmist opens as with a roll of drums (*verse* 1).

Because this psalm is so lofty in its thought and searching in its analysis men have always felt that only the greatest of the sons of men could speak such words. Thus the Hebrews attributed the psalm to Moses. But the superscriptions of the psalms have no historical value, and the superscription here which ascribes it to Moses is not in accord with the initial and later parts of the psalm which plainly looks back over a long stretch of Hebrew history (verses 1, 15). Hebrew religious thought had a long course of growth and development and the thought represented here is that of the later period: such ripeness and maturity come not at the beginning but in the process of time and in the succession of the generations.

Most commentators interpret the psalm in terms of modern thought and find a vein of pathos and romanticism here. Such a mood is common enough in modern poets but it did not come naturally to the austere Hebrew, and it is not present here. We have, indeed, thoughts that seem to skirt the very edge of pessimism, and might well lead the poet down to the abyss where men say, "All is vanity." Swinburne and William Morris and Ecclesiastes speak so, but the native Hebrew was saved from the final descent by a deep underlying faith and a fierce moral earnestness. Ecclesiastes is not typical Hebrew, for he represents the Hebrew genius crossed with the Greek, and in him we have a mongrel thing, "sicklied o'er with the pale cast of thought." The Psalmist was not so: he may have doubts at times, but in the light of his initial certainty, which he never lets go, all doubts are resolved. The Everlasting Nay is finally overcome by the Everlasting Yea.

Kittel tells us there are two contrasts here in this psalm, the contrast between God and man, and the contrast between God and Sin. But that, in a manner, is too objective, and it may be wiser to follow Weiser's treatment and regard the matter more subjectively. Thus we will set the contrast in the moods of the singer's mind. The first contrast will then be in the region of thought and emotion, while the second will be in the region of conscience and will. The last part of the psalm (verses 13–17) will represent and declare how those contrasts are finally removed and dissonances disappear in the final asurance of the omnipotent grace of God. Thus the psalm will divide naturally into three parts (1–6; 7–12; 13–17), and the thought will be seen to move in a spiral form from darkness to light, from defeat to victory, from earth to heaven.

i

The opening verses with their elevated language show the theocentric emphasis of the psalm. This is maintained throughout and never lost. Against the background of the eternal God is set the frailty and transience of man. The eternity of God is set forth in the only form available to the Hebrew, not abstractly but concretely and definitely. "As old as the hills" we say when we wish to describe something very ancient and of high antiquity, and that is how the Hebrew speaks. His God is older than "the everlasting hills": before they were born he was there and he will be there when they are no more. The hills are old but God is older far.

From age to age thou art God (*El*).

Old mythological ideas may lie behind these expressions, but there are depths in that last phrase concerning God's everlasting being which no human plummet can fathom. Against all the transience of man he stands fast for ever. The Psalmist is not lamenting man's apparent weakness and frailty, as modern writers do, but is centering upon the greatness of his God, and using man's littleness to show forth God's greatness (verses 3, 4). God reigns supreme, and he does his will among the armies of heaven and on the earth. At his word men are recalled to whence they came, and dust returns to dust. The text of verse 5 seems slightly overloaded metrically and may be corrupt. Duhm gives a lively rendering, by a slight alteration of the consonantal text, and this may well be right:

> Thou sowest them year by year,
> As springing grass are they:
>
> In the morning it springs flourishing
> At evening time it withers and fades.

Like the grass on the house-top, blasted by the blazing sun, so soon withered and gone—such is man. "All flesh is grass and all the goodliness thereof as the flower of the field." In many a metaphor and striking similitude the Hebrew sets forth the frailty and weakness of man, not because he is weak and frail, but that he may set forth the greatness of Almighty God.

> The One remains, the many change and pass;
> Heaven's light for ever shines, Earth's shadows fly:
> Life, like a dome of many-colored glass.
> Stains the white radiance of eternity,
> Until death tramples it to fragments.
>
> (SHELLEY, *Adonais*)

But the thought of Shelley here is anthropocentric, while the thought of the poet here is wholly theocentric.

Such reflections might well lead to a deep pessimism, and, if Hebrew thought had been as modern thought, it would have issued in despair. But such an issue is not here, for over against this transience of mortal men the writer sets the everlasting God. God abides. Man's frailty is but the foil to set forth the eternity of God. The issue in Ecclesiastes is sheer pessimism that can only say, "Vanity of vanities, all is vanity." The poet here is saved from that descent, and this must be emphasised here, for most expositors have over-stressed the emotional and sentimental aspect of the psalm and have regarded the singer as a modern romanticist. Here we have not the pessimism that characterised the later period of Hebrew history but only sheer realism. The poet looks at things as they are and measures them with no human standard. He lifts them into the light of the eternal and examines them *sub specie aeternitatis*. Others, including Ecclesiastes, may look at the same things and interpret them in the light of a *carpe diem* philosophy, which can only say: "Let us eat, drink, and be merry, for tomorrow we die." Such an attitude was impossible to the poet, and, if Ecclesiastes had maintained his Hebrew heritage unimpaired, it would have been impossible for him also.

ii

In the second section the poet moves further and probes deeper. The contrast now is not in the region of thought and emotion but in the realm of conscience and the will. The contrast is not between two kinds of being, transient and eternal, but between two wills, the will of God and the will of man. Here the divine is seen standing over against the human, and it stands in judgment and condemnation. For the poet feels that the brevity of life is bound up with ethical and religious facts. The writer may not say exactly as Paul says, "The wages of sin is death," but that is certainly

the direction in which his thought is moving. Man's transience is due to the divine wrath, and that wrath is stirred by
the sight of man's sin (*verses* 7–9).

> Our years come to end like a sigh!
>
> (VERSE 9)

Few phrases are more familiar than the words of the Authorised Version:

> We spend our years as a tale that is told,
>
> (VERSE 9)

but the Hebrew is much more expressive than that familiar
phrase, and the American Version has rendered more precisely. The Greek Version reads "like a spider's web," and
that is striking enough, but the Hebrew word here should be
noted. It is the word *Hegeh,* used of the psalmist's medita-
tion in Psalm 1:2, used of the fierce muttering of the rebels
in Psalm 2:1, used also of the moaning of doves (Isaiah
59:11), and also of wizards that cheep and mutter (Isaiah
8:19). It is a word associated with necromancy where all is
apt to be dubious, tenuous, and dark. Life is as insubstantial
as all that. The Greek evidently read the word *gūgāh* and is
followed by the Syriac: life may be as fine-spun as a spider's
web which crashes at the first rude blow from without. Both
figures are possible to the Hebrew poet, but perhaps "like a
sigh" accords better with what we find elsewhere in Scripture. "Your life is but a vapor," says James (James 4:14),
and that thought is echoed in many literatures and finds a
ready response in our hearts today. But why should life
seem so? Why should we have this bleak and bare prospect?
Why should we spend our years in thy wrath? The writer
undoubtedly has in mind the tragic story of man's fall as
set forth in Genesis 3, and over all life there lies the sombre
shadow of death, for, as Paul says, "The carnal mind is
enmity against God." The psalmist looks at man, and, as he

looks, his mood changes from wonder at God's greatness
(verses 2–6) to terror at his judgment. God's judgment is
revealed and made clear to man in the brevity and frustration of human life. Life is hopeless as it is because it is life
without God, and life without God holds no prospect. The
"lie is in the soul" of man, and all his life is hollow and
empty. Our secret sins which we hug to our bosom he sets
in the startling light of his countenance: the fierce light that
beats upon the Great White Throne reveals those sins of
ours for what they really are, and "all our days decline in
thy wrath." Life is "bound in shallows and in miseries," and
we fail to find a meaningful pattern of life. Our best efforts
are doomed to frustration and defeat because our fundamental attitude is wrong. Our strength at its best is but "toil
and futility": here the poet use words that are heavy and
weighted with despair. Surely "the sting of death is sin,"
and all sin, as Augustine has made clear, is the preferring of
one's own will to the will of God.

That is the root of the human tragedy. But the psalmist
knows it need not be so. Another attitude to life is possible,
and that other attitude can set life in tune with the Infinite
and redeem life from futility. A meaningful pattern of life
can be found if man will only think, if out of all his experiences he can extract experience and become wise unto salvation. But man goes on his way uncomprehending and
unheeding: he reckons not of his sin and the judgment of
God. Verse 11, following a suggestion of the Greek Version,
should be translated more exactly:

> Who knows the power of thine anger?
> And who stands in awe of thy wrath?

This restores the exact Hebrew parallelism and clarifies
the thought. Religion is at a discount among men: men are
refusing to take God seriously. If they think of his wrath it
is only as a bogey to be lightly dismissed. It does not enter

into life as a real factor and motivating power. But the
psalmist knows, in his heart he knows, that it is religion that
gives the proper perspective in this matter, and that religion
can sanctify life and fill it with significance. These men have
not "the fear of God" before their eyes: they have left God
out of all their thoughts. Like Gallio they "cared for none of
these things" (Acts 18:17). The psalmist knows that it is
only as man renounces all his own efforts and casts himself
in faith on the everlasting God, making God's will the rule
of his life, that he will find the meaningful way of life which
is beyond all transience and frailty. This alone will yield the
deep satisfactions that man requires. Only thus can life get
a new set and a new setting where doubt and despair are
swallowed up in abiding joy (verse 12). Only God can give
the capacity for this new view and strength for the new life.
We are saved by grace, and that not of ourselves. Man then
sees life from a new viewpoint, for he has harvested a heart
of wisdom. Life is no longer measured by human standards,
but is seen and lived "under the eyes and by the blessing of
God," and all time is redeemed.

...

iii

So we have the closing prayer (13–17). Most commentators are inclined to regard this part as not homogeneous
with what has preceded and would regard it as a separate
piece. This is unnecessary. There is a remarkable unity of
spirit here. For that prayer is not a prayer for self but for
others. It is not a prayer for material goods but for spiritual
and inward grace. It is marked by a strange urgency that
always inheres in faith that is really vital (verse 13). Faith
may grow impatient at times, but it is always certain of its
hope and trust. The certainty expressed in the first verse
abides throughout. Everything depends on the divine grace.
It is grace that makes the new attitude possible, and through
grace the contrast between God and man, formerly expressed

in judgment, is now resolved in a higher unity. Judgment and mercy come to light, but judgment is swallowed up of mercy and grace reigns. As men bow before God and yield their selfish wills God raises and exalts them. Judgment and mercy meet together: righteousness and truth kiss each other, and God is revealed as "a just God *and* a Savior" (Isaiah 45:21). For such a revelation the psalmist prays, that the transient life of mortal men may become illumined with the light of the Eternal and get imperishable significance. Grace reigns. By God's grace man's work, formerly meaningless and full of futility, becomes meaningful and established, because it is now part and parcel of the divine will. The life that in its noblest efforts seemed only "toil and futility" now becomes purposive and intelligent because it is charged with the divine. Illusion gives place to reality, transience to permanence, the Everlasting Nay to the Everlasting Yea, and faith finds its final expression in the opening word, "thou hast been our refuge through all generations."

> O with thy tender mercies, Lord,
>   us early satisfy:
> So we rejoice shall all our days,
>   and still be glad in thee.
>
> According as the days have been
>   wherein we grief have had,
> And years wherein we ill have seen,
>   so do thou make us glad.
>
> O let thy work and power appear
>   thy servants' face before,
> And show unto our children dear
>   thy glory evermore.
>
> And let the beauty of the Lord
>   our God be us upon:
> Our handiworks establish thou,
>   establish them each one.
>
> (*Verses* 13–17: Metrical Version)

The writer makes no apology for quoting this prayer in the

metrical form, for it has been graven on his memory and heart from earliest days. There is something haunting and indescribably tender about the thought in this form that makes it almost exceed the original in wistful pathos and noble passion. Here we have man's peaceful assent to the *Everlasting Yea.*

14

A SONG OF NATIONAL THANKSGIVING

PSALM 124

THE TESTIMONY OF ISRAEL

1 If *it had not been* the Lord who was on our side,
  now may Israel say;

2 If *it had not been* the Lord who was on our side,
  when men rose up against us:

3 Then they had swallowed us up quick,
  when their wrath was kindled against us:

4 Then the waters had overwhelmed us,
  the stream had gone over our soul.

5 Then the proud waters had gone over our soul.

6 Blessed *be* the Lord,
  who hath not given us *as* a prey to their teeth.

7 Our soul is escaped as a bird out of the snare of the
    fowlers:
  the snare is broken and we are escaped.

8 Our help is in the name of the Lord,
  who made heaven and earth.

This song has been cited earlier in the Metrical Version on pages 6–7. It is a favorite psalm with the Scots as one might expect, for they, like the Jews, have had a sufficient share of battles and wars and, full many a time, have they had occasion to praise God for victory given. Not once or twice "in their rough island story" has this psalm formed the song of national thanksgiving. For such a song is this psalm and strangely enough there is only one other of this type (Psalm 129). It would seem as if the Jew put all he had into this song and he needed no more.

This same song made a strong appeal to Luther who also had a full share of battle and strife. We can understand how he would find ample relief in the spacious tones of this vigorous song of thanksgiving. This song of Luther's is not as well known as *Ein feste Burg ist unser Gott,* for that hymn is unique in that it excels the original Hebrew in strength and power. In the Lutheran Church hymnal the song is ascribed to Luther but it would seem that in its composition he was assisted by Justus Jonas. Several translations have been made of the German *War Gott nicht mit uns diese Zeit,* and that in most frequent use is by R. Massie. But we prefer the translation given in the Lutheran Hymnal (Missouri Synod):

> If God had not been on our side
> and had not come to aid us,
> The foes with all their pow'r and pride
> would surely have dismayed us:
> For we, His flock, would have to fear
> the threats of men both far and near
> who rise in might against us.
>
> Their furious wrath, did God permit,
> Would surely have consumed us,
> And as a deep and yawning pit
> With life and limb entombed us.

Like men o'er whom dark waters roll
   Their wrath would have engulfed our soul,
   And like a flood o'erwhelmed us.
Blest be the Lord who foiled their threat,
   That they could not devour us;
Our souls, like birds, escaped their net,
   They could not overpow'r us:
The snare is broken—we are free!
   Our help is ever, Lord, in Thee,
   Who madest earth and heaven.

This version exceeds the Scots version in poetical quality but for vigor and vitality the Scots version is superior.

No date can be set upon this psalm. It sings of a situation that recurred time and again in the history of Israel. It might be taken as referring to the exodus from Egypt when the stretched-out arm and mighty hand of Israel's God cast the horse and his rider into the sea and led Israel safely to the dry land. That was a day Israel never did forget and this song with its triumphant note might well commemorate that great day in the national life. Or it could refer to the Exile and the Return from Babylon or yet again it might be later still—Duhm refers it to the days of John Hyrcanus in the Maccabean period. That it was some great and perilous venture is clear from the moving tones and vivid pictures in which the deliverance is portrayed. The slight Aramaic flavor about the language might suggest a later date but it could refer to that time in the life of Isaiah when "the Assyrian came down like the wolf on the fold" and "the overflowing scourge" threatened the kingdom of Judah. The range of possible reference is wide, for all Israel's history was full of God and sacramental. Time and again those mighty deliverances had revealed the character of God and Israel knew Jehovah as a God of compassion and endless mercy. As they recalled those holy memories to mind and reviewed their national history they were constrained to

praise God for his unceasing grace and his mighty deliverances.

The greatness and the goodness of God in his salvation
are set forth in a description of what might have been if
Jehovah had not sustained them when cruel men rose up
against them. The graphic nature of this description and its
shuddering horror at what might have become of them
shows the magnitude of the deliverance and the greatness
of Jehovah who delivered them. Those nations that marched
and counter-marched up and down the *Via Maris,* from
Egypt to Assyria and Assyria to Egypt, with nothing to
serve but their own hot, greedy, snatching appetites—they
were gone, gone for ever, but Israel remained. Israel remained by the marvelous grace of God and Israel still remains. For Israel had something they had not. They had no
truth, no righteousness, no mercy, but these things were
central in Israel's God and they were central in Israel the
people of God. Well may George Adam Smith [1] say of
Israel: "The sheer vitality of the breed, both physical and
spiritual, has been so intense and, despite demoralisations
and disasters sufficient to have shattered other peoples, has
been so enduring as to imply sources of blood and of brain
uncommonly rich and vigorous."

And so Israel remained and still remains because, despite
all their failures and demoralisations, there was a spiritual
principle at the center of the national life. Those other
nations were merely material forces compounded of physical
power and animal instincts; their unity and coherence were
by physical bonds and, when these were burst and broken,
they melted away and were buried in the dust. Israel was no
military empire, but it excelled in the things of the spirit
and it has endured because its unity and coherence are due
to a spiritual bond which cannot be dissolved by the things

[1] *The Legacy of Israel,* p. 2.

of time. They had what those others had not, a God with character who called them to walk in the way of spiritual distinction.

All that is clear in the song as they sing of their deliverance and praise their mighty God. What a deliverance! Beastly powers—do we libel the beasts in so saying?—like those huge monsters of the vasty deep that sought to swallow up the people of God alive (Jeremiah 51:34), fearful and threatening like the crashing rushing waters of the wadies in time of winter—or is the singer thinking of the waters of the underworld? — and cunning as the crafty snarers and entrappers of birds—was he thinking here of Sennacherib who "shut up Hezekiah in Jerusalem like a bird in a cage"?—from them all we are escaped away by the wondrous mercy of our God. Blessed be his great and holy name. As the English people, after the victory over the Spanish Armada, met in their churches to praise God and sing this old psalm they commemorated the wonderful deliverance by striking a medal on which was inscribed the words, *Deus afflavit et dissipati sunt* (God blew and they were scattered). This psalm in Scotland is often called "Durie's Psalm" in memory of the fact that when brave John Durie defied the high-handed acts of James VI, as Sennacherib defied Hezekiah, the whole town of Edinburgh turned out to greet the brave pastor and escorted him through the city as they sang "till heaven and earth resounded,"

Now Israel may say and that trewly.

Likewise in Geneva, when the Dukes of Savoy sought to crush the Reform Movement and in 1602 had stolen secretly upon the city, they were balked in the attempt by what might seem to many a matter of chance, but by what the Reformers interpreted as a *Providentia specialissima.* Theodore Beza, then eighty years old, returned the nation's thanks in the words of this psalm. So sang the Jews and in singing so they revealed their lofty thought of God.

> Except Jehovah build the house,
> They labor in vain that build it:
> Except Jehovah keep the city,
> The watchman waketh but in vain.
>
> (PSALM 127:1)

If God is for us he is more than all that be against us. Of ourselves we can do nothing: our help and our hope is in him. That was the faith of the Hebrews and that is the secret of their survival. They believed in a God who was big enough to make the world and all therein, and they believed in a God good enough to make spiritual principles regulatory of his world.

> Our help is in the name of the Lord,
> Who made heaven and earth.
>
> (VERSE 7)

Thus memory kindled hope and faith was fortified by experience.

15

A PROPHETIC PSALM

PSALM 82

THE JUDGMENT OF THE GODS

1 God standeth in the congregation of the mighty:
  he judgeth among the gods.

2 How long will ye judge unjustly,
  and accept the persons of the wicked?

3 Defend the poor and the fatherless:
  do justice to the afflicted and needy.

4 Deliver the poor and needy:
  rid *them* out of the hand of the wicked.

5 They know not, neither will they understand:
  they walk on in darkness;
  all the foundations of the earth are out of course.

6 I have said, Ye are gods:
  and all of you are children of the Most High:

7 But ye shall die like men,
  and fall like one of the princes.

8 Arise, O God, judge the earth:
  for thou shalt inherit all nations.

"No psalm makes a stronger demand than this on the historic imagination of the interpreter." So says Cheyne, and we may well give heed to his word. For here we have something quite unique in the Psalter. Indeed this imaginative flight has been too much for most commentators and it has been subjected to prosaic and pedestrian interpretation. In its combination of prophetic doctrine and mythological coloring we have a song that is quite unusual. With a wondrous flight of fancy we are lifted "into the heavenlies" and presented with such a scene as meets us in the first chapter of the book of Job, where all the ministering heavenly spirits come together to give account of their stewardship to Jehovah. It is precisely this idea of a host of lesser deities constituting the court of heaven that proves repugnant to commentators. But it must be borne in mind that the lofty monotheism which finds expression in such a prophet as Isaiah of the Exile was not the common possession of the multitude. It was not even in the mind of this poet. Men were then groping and seeking their way toward such a full idea, and this song represents one of the steps in that forward march. For the Psalter represents Hebrew piety in its growth and development: all its teaching is not on the level of Psalm 51 or 139.

The failure to recognise this fact has led many scholars to see in "the congregation of the mighty," which may be more correctly rendered "the congregation of God (*El*)," not gods, but earthly judges. This interpretation has behind it the authority of the Jewish Targum and would seem to be supported by an apparently similar reference in Exodus 21:6. But that is not really so, for the reference in that passage is to *gods* and is so interpreted by most commentators. In the present psalm we are dealing with monolatry but not monotheism, and while we have here a dualistic view of things, that was not the final view of the Old Testa-

ment. It was a stage in the development. It would appear
here that the singer is concerned with the general problem
of suffering, and is seeking, as others sought, to account for
obvious moral anomalies. Why do the innocent suffer, and
why do the wicked prosper? Because, he answers, the guardian deities, to whom the oversight of the world has been
entrusted by God, have proved unfaithful in the discharge
of their appointed task. They have failed to reveal such
character as might have been expected; they have "fallen
down on the job," and, therefore, rampant injustice fills the
earth.

i

Now that may not be a native Hebrew idea. It may be an
adopted belief taken over from an alien environment. There
is no need to deny the presence of such ideas in our Old
Testament. It would be difficult to explain verse 7 of this
psalm on any other basis than that of lesser deities or guardian angels standing in the presence of God and called upon
to execute his sovereign will. Moreover, it would be easy
for a poet to think and speak in this way, for polytheism
affords much more scope to poetic imagination than does a
rigorous monotheism. Here we see in operation that process
by which the thought of Israel passed from polytheism to a
real belief in one God. That this polytheistic and mythological background meets us elsewhere in the Old Testament
is clear from various references. Micaiah ben Yimla, the
prophet, tells us of the court of heaven and how things are
arranged there to attain the divine end (I Kings 22:19):
there spirits stand ready to speed over land and sea to do
the bidding of Jehovah. We see it, as already mentioned, in
the book of Job (1:6ff.; 2:1; 15:8), and the same thought
appears frequently in the Psalter (Psalm 8:6; 29:1; 89:7).
This may be due to Israel's inheritance of an alien mythol-

ogy, or, in the later period, it may be due to a process of rationalisation. Deutero-Isaiah may assert the non-existence of heathen deities—and such assertion is necessary in the case of a thoroughgoing monotheism — but others thought of those deities in a different way. Those others did not deny their reality but they did assert the supremacy of Israel's God over every other deity. Those deities were stripped of their divinity and reduced to the position of ministering servants of the Almighty God. They exist only to do his will. From that idea, in large measure, developed and grew the angelology of Judaism, though other influences may have facilitated that development which is found in advanced form in the book of Daniel with its doctrine of guardian angels (Daniel 10:13, 20, 21). The Greek text of Deuteronomy 32:8 diverges in a remarkable way from the Hebrew text and most scholars regard the Greek as being closer to the original. It reads as follows:

> When the Most High gave to the nations their
>   inheritance,
> When he separated the children of men,
> He set the bounds of the peoples
> According to the number of the sons of God.

Similarly in Deuteronomy 4:19 and 29:25, as in Ecclesiasticus 17:17 and Isaiah 24:21, we meet with this same suggestion that each nation has its guardian deity in heaven. Furthermore, in the book of Daniel we have the thought that the troubles and disorders of earth are due to divisions and counsels among the guardian deities in heaven (Daniel 10:13, 20, 21). The thought of such a judgment as is here portrayed appears to lie behind the denunciation of heathen gods in Deutero-Isaiah (41:21ff.; 44:7ff.; 45:20ff.). It need not surprise us, therefore, to find such a thought in the present psalm.

In the present instance the poet seems to be dealing with

the general question of theodicy, the justifying of the ways
of God with men. This question exercised some of the greatest minds in the Old Testament, and has given rise to some
of its noblest literature, the book of Job and Psalm 73 and
Isaiah 53. Here the poet is seeking a solution for the question that vexed him: why are such cruelties and oppressions
possible in a world ruled by a righteous God? He finds the
answer in the fact that the guardian deities appointed for
man's welfare have failed to show understanding and have
lacked insight. They have been remiss and negligent in the
discharge of their duties, and consequently the moral foundations of life are crumbling. There may be no real solution
here and the problem may only be pushed back with the
introduction of this thought of dualism, but the divine righteousness is not impugned, as in Job, but rather vindicated
and maintained. It is this same thought that later finds
expression in the idea of Satan as a personal evil power
opposed to God, which finds its fuller form in the thought
of the New Testament devil (*diabolos*). None of these ways
may provide an adequate solution for the problem but they
all betoken a moral earnestness and effort to vindicate the
character of God and maintain the spiritual basis of life.
The Psalmist knows that the righteousness of God will be
finally revealed, and that his faith in the uniqueness of his
God will be confirmed.

The psalm is designated by Gunkel as *a prophetic imita-
tion*. It might be classed with the Wisdom songs and associated with Psalms 37, 49, 58, 73. Duhm would set it in the
period of the Hasmoneans and regards it as a psalm of the
Pharisees. This is altogether improbable and we will not be
far astray if we date it after the Exile when Israel was suffering from foreign oppression.

The form of the song is simple enough, and the metre is
regular except for a variation in verse 5, which many com-

mentators would regard, in whole or in part, as the marginal
comment of a scribe. The opening verse sets the scene in
style similar to that of the first chapter of Job; the discussion is in heaven while the drama is on earth. The main
piece (2–7) sets forth *the great arraignment* and the divine
sentence, while the psalm closes with an eschatological hope,
as is common in the prophets.

ii

> God takes his stand in the divine assembly,
> In the midst of the gods he judges.
>
> (VERSE 1)

So we must translate the first verse. Men think of the
divine court in terms of the earthly. As the Persian king was
wont to call his satraps around him and hear an account of
their stewardship so does God in the court of heaven. A task
has been given them and a responsibility entrusted to his
servants and now they are called to give account. There is a
spirit of tension and expectancy here and a strange economy
of words. All has not been as it should be, but God has been
marvelously patient. His patience, however, is at an end,
and now he comes to judge. There is something ominous and
threatening in those words, and like a storm the divine
rebuke breaks upon the heads of those guardian deities
(verse 2). Those representatives of the inflexibly righteous
God have turned aside from the *straight path*, which is the
Hebrew concrete expression for impartial justice. They have
made it winding and twisting, and God's children have been
forced to cry, "How long, O Lord, how long?" It would seem
as if that impatient cry was ringing in the ears of God when
he advances to judgment (verses 3, 4). The almost monoto-
nous repetition of such injunctions, not only in the Psalter
but throughout the Old Testament, is a sad commentary on
human nature and throws a flood of light on ancient society.

Somehow religion, which is a community affair, never seems
to find adequate social expression, and from the day of
Israel's settlement in Canaan we never cease to hear the cry
of the under-privileged. Doubtless there were those who
were responsible for their own poverty—the book of Prov-
erbs does not overlook that fact—but the mass of destitu-
tion and poverty prevalent in ancient Israel would indicate
a very large measure of "man's inhumanity to man." From
the days of Amos we see this festering sore in the life of the
community; the "poor are sold for a pair of shoes" (Amos
2:6) and the under-privileged are exploited more and more.
Micah and Isaiah bewail the same sad circumstances, and
all are agreed that the fundamental lack is a lack of righteousness (Amos 5:23ff.; Isaiah 1:14–17). This is the burden
on the soul of the prophet and the psalmist. Equal-handed
justice, which is the stay and strength of any community,
was far to seek in those days. The poor were growing poorer,
and the afflicted more distressed, and so it will always be
when justice is sold for money. There the "survival of the
slickest" becomes the rule of life, and its law is the law of
the jungle. The social problem, as we call it, becomes sharp-
ened to an intolerable point of agony.

But, though this state of affairs prevailed, it must not be
overlooked or forgotten that an unceasing protest is made
by those who speak for Israel's God. Elijah will stand before
Ahab to lay bare the atrocity of Naboth's murder (I Kings
21), and Nathan will set forth, in parable form, the utter
meanness of the king who had Uriah killed and stole his
wife (II Samuel 12). Amos, too, will confront Amaziah in
the royal sanctuary at Bethel and will tell him to his face
that rites avail not at all if right be absent (Amos 7:14f.).
In all these instances we are dealing with expressions of the
central spirit of Hebrew religion. Righteousness is set in the
very heart of God, and he is righteous altogether and loves

righteousness. Everything in earth and heaven must conform to this righteousness. It is precisely this fusion of religion and ethics that links together the service of God and the service of man: righteousness is not only a divine attribute but also a human duty. This it was that gained for Judaism the respect of the ancient world, and this, too, it was that Christianity took over to embody in its own ethic, expressed in the great commandment:

> Thou shalt love the Lord thy God . . . and thy
> neighbor as thyself.
>
> (LUKE 10:27)

iii

The Old Testament does not have the word "religion." But it has a few significant synonyms. *Knowledge of God* is one of these, and it occurs here. Where there is no knowledge of God, of what God really is and what God requires, there will be moral confusion and social maladjustment. And so we have that situation set forth in verse 5. There is bitter irony in these words, as there is irony in similar words of Deutero-Isaiah. Gods without insight! What a travesty of divinity is here! It might seem as if we could read between the lines a repudiation of polytheism, for how should alien gods know or have insight into the will and purpose of the righteous God of Israel? They thought he was "altogether such an one as they." But Israel's God is unique, and he dwells alone: none can be compared with him.

> For who in heaven can be compared unto
> the Lord? *who* among the sons of the
> mighty can be likened unto the Lord?
>
> (PSALM 89:6)

He is Incomparable and has no peer (Isaiah 40:25). Little wonder is it that the world is thrown into confusion and commotion through their lack of knowledge and insight.

Their spiritual failure has repercussions in the realm of Nature, for, to the Hebrew, the moral and natural worlds were one and interwoven.

It is to be noted that those deities make no reply. That may be due to the Hebrew poetic genius, which is characterised by intense subjectiveness. It may be an expression of prophetic irony intended to suggest that they are but "dumb dogs that cannot bark." But there is new hope for men. Those gods have been tried and found wanting. Events have shown them for what they really are, and now is declared what they shall be. Once they were clothed with dignity and given high office, but now they are depotentiated and thrust down from their lofty sphere (verses 6, 7). Verse 7 makes clear that it is no class of human beings with which we are concerned here. These belong to the higher sphere and share a higher type of being. But they have failed, and sore travail has come upon men through their failure. But the dawn is at hand for all that are oppressed. God holds judgment in heaven: he has arisen to put things right. Righteousness is about to be revealed. Thus the poet has hope, and breathes his prayer—which some scholars reject as an interpolation—that God may arise and reign (verse 8). The righteous God will do righteously, and earth will own his sway.

PART III

THE RELIGIOUS TEACHING OF THE PSALTER

16

THE THOUGHTS OF MANY HEARTS

It seems desirable to speak here of religious teaching rather than the theology of the Psalter. For here we are concerned with a devotional literature that represents the distilled piety of countless generations. Here we are dealing with the outpouring of the human heart rather than with a system of reasoned ideas. Joy here is too abounding and sorrow is too passionate to be compressed within the molds of a logical system. If we seek to analyse the experiences of the saints in too minute fashion, we may find the spirit itself eluding our search and, like those who would "break a butterfly on the wheel," we may miss the very thing we seek to find. For "the heart has its reasons which the reason cannot know," [1] and nowhere is that more true than in the present connection.

One or two preliminary matters may be referred to before we proceed to examine the religious teaching of the Psalter. In the first place one might well question whether it is possible to extract from those varied spiritual experiences any

[1] Pascal, Blaise, *Pensées,* Sec. 4:277.

consistent scheme of thought. For the book is the deposit of religious thought through many centuries and does not spring from one particular period, though in the main it may represent the piety of post-exilic Judaism. Nevertheless, though there are certainly variations in the religious viewpoint and a growth and development in theological thought, the fundamental religious experiences and the human reactions are the same throughout the Psalter. For the human heart does not change in its essential demands and responses. Where formal variations occur they may be noted and registered, but caution must be employed here. For, frequently, in the sphere of religion crude ideas will be found persisting alongside more developed conceptions, and a saint may even appear as "one born out of due season" and far ahead of his time. We may not seek to regulate the working of the divine spirit or to foreclose the possibilities of revelation.

Furthermore, the Psalter deals with religious experience and is concerned with human life in its relation to God. In one sense we have here less of the word of God and more of the word of man. It might appear as if, in comparison with the prophetic literature, we are dealing with something of less value. For here, in large measure, we have to do with man's reflections on the ways of God rather than with God's own word that comes to the prophet with constraining power that makes him say "Thus saith the Lord." But those singers are not so far removed from the seers of Israel, for those psalmists "spake as they were moved by the Holy Spirit," and the reflections to which they give utterance owe their origin to divine prompting. If we desire to make a distinction, we might say the prophets were moved from without while the psalmists were moved from within. But such a distinction might well be questioned. There is no real difference here, for the prophetic oracle was colored and mediated

by the prophet's own mind. Again, it may be asserted that
the prophets moved more in the realm of thought and action
while the psalmists were more occupied with feeling and
emotion. But religious feeling requires guidance no less than
religious thought. Thus if it be true, as Keble asserts in the
introduction to *The Christian Year,* that "next to a sound
rule of faith" nothing is so necessary as "a sober standard
of feeling," we shall set no small store by the revelation that
comes to us in the inspired songs of the Psalter. For here we
learn the real meaning of communion with God, and we
attain to "a sober standard of feeling."

a. *The Psalmist's Thought of God*

The Old Testament never argues about the existence of
God: that is its primary assumption. He is the "self-evident
presupposition of every beginning." God does not need to be
explained, but without him the world is inexplicable.

"In the beginning God" is the first word of the Hebrew
Scriptures: here is the initial premise of all his thought. The
being of God is the fundamental presupposition which is
never debated or denied but steadily maintained throughout
the Old Testament. Foolish men (Psalm 14:1, 53:2, Jeremiah 5:12) and foolish women (Job 2:10) may appear to
assert the contrary but in so doing they reveal their folly:
they are so sunken in evil ways that they may no longer be
considered worthy of the name of men. They are "corrupt"
(Psalm 14:1, 53:1) and "brutish" (Psalm 94:8): their ungodly conduct has blinded them to moral realities:

> The wicked, through the pride of his countenance,
> will not seek after God: all his thoughts are, there
> is no God.
>
> (PSALM 10:4)

This is practical atheism, not theoretical: the Old Testament knows nothing of theoretical atheism. The Psalmist

wastes little time in argument of a theological kind; that was not the Hebrew way. But in Psalm 94 he does address the "brutish" as if they had understanding:

> Understand, ye brutish among the people:
> and *ye fools,* when will ye be wise?
> He that planted the ear, shall he not hear?
> he that formed the eye, shall he not see?
> He that chastiseth the heathen, shall not he correct?
> Even he that teacheth man knowledge?
>
> (PSALM 94:8–10)

The Hebrew begins with God. The godly cry to him and are heard by him (Psalm 34:4), all the peoples praise him (117:1), fire and hail, wind and snow, mountains and all hills, creeping things and flying fowl, princes and commoners, old and young (Psalm 148:8–12), praise him who is the ground of their being. Among all the nations his name is magnified (Malachi 1:11). All alike acknowledge "that God is, and that he is a rewarder of them that diligently seek him" (Hebrews 11:6). On that foundation the life of the godly is built.

Our next concern must be with the character or nature of God. With reference to the question of monotheism we must have in mind the *caveat* expressed in the beginning of this discussion and guard against the temptation to force the thoughts expressed by these singers into a cast-iron theological mold. If by monotheism we mean *an expressed belief in one God with expressed denial of all other gods* then such monotheism will be hard to find in the Psalter. These singers had no exact theological viewpoint, and such monotheism as we have just defined may not be found before the time of "Isaiah" of the Exile (Isaiah 40–55). He is both a theologian and a religious philosopher. It may be that monotheism is clearly implied in such passages as Psalms 115:4–8; 135:15–17, but that is not general. Frequently, indeed, we have the opposite of monotheism implied and expressed.

Who is a great God like unto God?

(PSALM 77:13)

There shall be no strange god in thee,
neither shalt thou worship any strange god.

(PSALM 81:9)

For the Lord is a great God,
and a great King above all gods.

(PSALM 95:3)

Psalm 82 suggests something far removed from monotheism, and examples of this might be multiplied. It may be in some instances that we are dealing with a poetic figure and the poet may be referring to these gods as we refer to the gods of Greece or Rome or India. If we can so speak without compromising our monotheism, the psalmist might well do the same. But when allowance is made for this—and quite large allowance may be made—there remains a large residue of cases that cannot be so explained. Thus we are forced to the conclusion that the Psalter contains many traces of a belief that falls considerably short of monotheism.

b. *The Names of God*

The names bestowed upon Israel's God are significant and worthy of note. To the Hebrews names were always real and meaningful; *nomina sunt realia*. The name itself was revealing. *El, Eloah, Elohim* are general terms and signify deity in general. These terms seem all to be derived from the same root, and the original meaning of the root may be either *strength* or *guidance*. Sellin and Eichrodt are inclined to adopt the latter meaning, but whether the original significance was *the Strong One* or *the Leader* all these terms emphasise the distance between man and God. *Elohim* in Köhler's [2] judgment goes back to a polytheistic stage, but Eichrodt [3] holds the polytheistic conception to be secondary. It is used in the Old Testament to signify both *God* and

---

[2] Köhler, Ludwig, *Theologie des Alten Testaments*, p. 18.
[3] Eichrodt, Walther, *Theologie des Alten Testaments*, Vol. I, p. 90.

gods, but its main use is in the singular reference and it usually takes the verb in the singular. It is thus to be regarded as an abstract plural, denoting an assemblage of powers in one person, or as we might otherwise put it, *a plural of majesty,* somewhat akin to the "imperial *we*" of an emperor or the "editorial *we*" of a newspaper editor. *El Elyon* (God Most High) meets us first in Genesis 14:18, where Melchizedek is described as "priest of the Most High God." This might suggest thoughts of monarchical polytheism, in which one God is elevated above all others. It is a favorite term in later writings, canonical and uncanonical, as it could be used to express the Jewish idea of monotheism without thrusting a name so strictly Jewish as *Yahwe* upon the heathen. But as used in the Psalter it expresses the sublime elevation of God. More archaic is the term *Shaddai,* translated *Almighty,* probably from the Assyrian word *Shadu,* meaning a mountain. God is the mighty and massive one. This term, like the others, indicates the elevation of God above humanity.

The most frequently occurring term is *Yahwe,* translated by the English Jehovah, and by the Greek Version as the *Lord,* which is followed by the Authorised Version. The word *Yahwe* occurs over 6700 times in the Old Testament. As to what the word meant originally no certainty is to be attained. Many conjectures have been made and we need not examine these. Sellin [4] holds the meaning to be "the eternally self-consistent," and this may well be what it signified to the Jews. The emphasis here is on the dynamic, not on the static aspects of deity, and the ceaseless activity of Israel's God is emphasised. It is the personal name of Israel's redeeming God, and there is about it something more intimate and personal than is expressed in the other terms. At times it may be set in combination with those

[4] Sellin, Ernst, *Theologie des Alten Testaments,* p. 8.

other terms to produce something particularly sonorous and impressive. *Yahwe Elohe Sabaoth,* Jehovah God of Hosts, is a frequent combination: the hosts may be the armies of Israel or the starry hosts, or yet again they may be the angelic hosts of heaven. In Psalm 50:1 we find *Yahwe El Elohim,* Yahwe, God of gods, and while most commentators are prepared to excise one or more of those terms there is no real reason for so doing. The term *Adon* is of uncertain etymology and is not properly a term for deity but rather an epithet. In the later period it was used almost exclusively for *Yahwe,* which word was regarded as too sacred to be uttered by human lips: in all passages where the word *Yahwe* stood in the text the Jew read the word *Adonay.* Like the other terms it expresses the idea of exaltation and elevation. "The chief point to be borne in mind is the surpassing excellence of that Being who unites in his person the glories to which so many glorious names severally testify." [5]

c. *The Attributes of God*

That God is Lord is the fundamental axiom of Old Testament theology. Köhler [6] refers to that as "the vertebral column of Old Testament theology." This we have seen expressed in the various names and titles of God. Now we come to consider the attributes of God, and in the first place we shall think of those which are generally called the metaphysical attributes. Not that the Hebrew thought in terms of metaphysic. But he was able to express in his own concrete way what we denote by such terms as eternity, omnipotence, omniscience, and omnipresence. When we seek to find the Hebrew form of expression for eternity we turn to Psalm 90:

[5] Davison, W. T., *The Praises of Israel,* p. 113.
[6] Köhler, Ludwig, *Theologie des Alten Testaments,* p. 17.

> Lord, thou has been our dwelling place in all
> generations.
> Before the mountains were brought forth, or
> ever thou hadst formed the earth and the
> world, even from everlasting to everlasting
> thou *art* God.

"As old as the hills," we say when we wish to express a high
degree of antiquity. That is to speak in the Hebrew way:
that is concrete and not abstract. My God, says the Hebrew,
is older than the hills: he was there before the hills were
formed and he will be there when the hills are no more.
That cuts through all our abstractions and speaks home to
the hearts of men. And not only is he eternal and omnipotent but he is also tender and gracious:

> He healeth the broken in heart and bindeth up
> their wounds.
> He telleth the number of the stars; he calleth
> them all by *their* names.
>
> (PSALM 147:3, 4)

It is this blending of grace and power that constrains the
singer to open his song with a loud "Hallelujah," for here
is ground for praise:

> Praise ye the Lord, for it is good to sing praises
> unto our God; for *it is* pleasant; and praise is
> comely.
>
> (PSALM 147:1)

And, as he opens, so he closes his song with another "Hallelujah" (Psalm 147:20).

Psalm 139 will show how wonderfully and graciously omniscience and omnipresence can be expressed:

> O Lord, thou hast searched me and known *me*.
> Thou knowest my down-sitting and mine up-
> rising,
> thou understandest my thought afar off.
> Thou compassest my path and my lying down,
> and art acquainted with all my ways.

For there is not a word in my tongue,
but lo, O Lord, thou knowest it altogether.
Thou hast beset me behind and before,
and laid thine hand upon me.
Such knowledge is too wonderful for me,
it is high, I cannot attain unto it.
Whither shall I go from thy Spirit?
or whither shall I flee from thy presence?
If I ascend up into heaven, thou art there:
if I make my bed in hell, behold thou *art there.*
If I take the wings of the morning
and dwell in the uttermost parts of the sea
Even there shall thy hand lead me,
and thy right hand shall hold me.
If I say, Surely the darkness shall cover me;
even the night shall be light about me.
Yea, the darkness hideth not from thee;
but the night shineth as the day:
the darkness and the light are both alike to
    thee.

(VERSES 1–12)

In such concrete fashion does the poet set forth the metaphysical attributes of God: he speaks of omniscience, omnipotence, omnipresence in language which a child may understand.

In terms no less simple are set forth the moral attributes
which display the essential goodness of God. The righteousness of God, his justice, his truth, his faithfulness, his goodness—these are the never-failing theme of the Psalmist.

Thy mercy, O Lord, is in the heavens;
    and thy faithfulness *reacheth* unto the clouds.

Thy righteousness is like the great mountains;
    thy judgments are a great deep:
    O Lord, thou preservest man and beast.

How excellent is thy loving-kindness, O God:
    therefore the children of men put their trust
    under the shadow of thy wings.

(PSALM 36:5–7)

There is no need to analyse these separate rays of the one great sun of moral and spiritual perfection. In God are united and blended in perfect proportion all moral and ethical perfections. Attention should, however, be called to the word translated *mercy* in verse 5 and *loving-kindness* in verse 7. This represents one and the same word in the original Hebrew. The varying rendering of the Authorised Version is due to the manifold content and meaning of the Hebrew term. That term is *Chesed,* usually translated in the Authorised Version by *loving-kindness.* George Adam Smith translated it in Hosea [7] as *leal love,* that is love that is loyal and true and firm, that can be relied upon under all circumstances. It is a favorite term with Hosea, most evangelical of the prophets, and the Authorized Version in Hosea has generally translated it by the English term *mercy.* But it is more than mercy or loving-kindness. It is a comprehensive word rooted in the ancient social structure, and it comes to us with "all the scents and murmurs of the infinite sea" upon it. For ancient life, as we see it in the pages of the Old Testament, was lived under the thought and reality of covenants. Life was possible under such protection. A man made a covenant with his wife, a master with his slave, a patron with his client, man with his fellow-man, and a people made a covenant with its God. The essence of such a covenant is *Chesed,* and without *Chesed* the covenant cannot be entered upon and cannot continue. *Chesed* is the loyalty which one member of a covenant owes to the other, a man to his wife, a master to his slave, a patron to his client, man to his brother man, and a nation to its God. Those relations are reciprocal and mutual. Without *Chesed* ordered communal life is not possible; when it is absent conditions become anarchical and "there is no truth, nor mercy (*Chesed*), nor knowledge of God in the land" (Hosea 4:1).

[7] *Expositor's Bible, The Book of the Twelve Prophets,* Vol. I.

Chesed is that on which all relationships, human and divine, ultimately rest. When *Chesed* is present there will be truth and righteousness and justice. It represents thus man's loyalty to God and God's loyalty and faithfulness to man, as also man's loyalty to his fellow-man. The term is wide and comprehensive as life itself. It is the basis of national solidarity and on it is grounded Israel's hope and confidence.

For the whole thought of the Old Testament moves within the framework of the Covenant made with Israel at Sinai. God made a covenant between himself and Israel, and between Yahwe and his people there is *Chesed*. That love and loyalty have been proved by his redemption of the people from the bondage of Egypt and by his subsequent guidance of their national history. But a covenant endures only as long as both parties are obedient to the terms of the covenant. If one party breaks the terms, it is no longer valid. In simple words the covenant made at Sinai was, "I will be to you a God and ye shall be to me a people." When Israel proved unfaithful to the covenant, and the righteous God was called upon to punish her, that was done in *Chesed*. For in judgment and chastisement the righteous God was seeking to restore the right covenant relation. That is the mood and view of the more profound spirits in Israel, as is seen, e.g., in Psalm 51. A more legalistic viewpoint is frequently apparent as, e.g., in Psalm 44. But the choicer spirits advanced to a viewpoint here which outran the original significance of *Chesed* as something obligatory and required by the nature of the covenant, and the term came to signify the free and undeserved mercy of God, the *loving-kindness* of verse 7 which in the Metrical Version is translated *grace* ("how precious is thy grace"). It thus became equivalent to the Hebrew *rachamim* (*compassion*) with which it is often combined in the Psalter. *Rachamim* is compassion to which one has no legal claim: it thus came to signify what we mean by *grace* and it may well denote what we mean by the *love of God*. Thus the psalmist comes to the point where he can say,

> the earth is full of the goodness (*Chesed*) of God
>
> (PSALM 35:5),
>
> the earth, O Lord, is full of thy mercy (*Chesed*)
>
> (PSALM 119:64),

that his *Chesed* is over all his works (Psalm 36:7; 145:9), and that Creation itself is a work of God's *Chesed* (136:1–9).

Thus the singers thought of God and so they spoke. This is the God of the Psalmists and though he be "throned on the praises of Israel" (Psalm 22:3) God is near to him that is of a contrite spirit (34:18). Man here is always aware of the majesty of his God, "a great king above all gods" (95:3), but he is also aware that God is near and ever ready to help. Devotion combines the *near God* and the *far God* into the God of glory and of grace.

> Who is like unto the Lord our God
>   who dwelleth on high,
> Who humbleth *himself* to behold
>   the heavens and the earth!
>
> (PSALM 113:5, 6)

Here is clearly seen how far men had traveled on the way of spiritual experience and how they were led to a fuller understanding of the intention of the divine heart. That the Almighty should humble himself is a somewhat surprising thought in the Old Testament though we are familiar with it in the New Testament (Philippians 2:5f.). Clearly men were coming to a deeper knowledge of the character of God, and the poet of Psalm 103 pierces to the roots and realities of things when he observes how the divine pity seems to be drawn down upon human weakness and frailty,

and how man's very feebleness seems to provoke and elicit
the divine compassion:

> Like as a father pitieth his children,
> so the Lord pitieth them that fear him.
> For.he knoweth our frame,
> he remembereth that we art dust.
>
> (PSALM 103:13, 14)

He is a God whose particular regard is extended to the suffering and the handicapped:

> The Lord openeth *the eyes of* the blind;
> the Lord raiseth them that are bowed down . . .
> The Lord preserveth the strangers:
> he relieveth the fatherless and the widow.
>
> (PSALM 146:8, 9)

> Thou tellest my wanderings: put my tears into
> thy bottle: *are they* not in thy book?
>
> (PSALM 56:8)

He is a God who counts the hairs of man's head, numbers
the beats of our hearts, and puts all our tears into his bottle.
Like a celestial physician he stands beside us in our sickness:

> The Lord will strengthen him upon the bed of
>   languishing,
> thou wilt make all his bed in his sickness.
>
> (PSALM 41:3)

He is a God who "thinketh on the poor and needy" (Psalm
40:17) and "though the Lord be high yet hath he respect
unto the lowly (138:6). Between these two poles of profound awe and reverence on the one side and simple trust
and confidence on the other lies the whole piety of the Old
Testament in general and of the Psalter in particular. This
we shall see more clearly as we proceed to examine the
Psalmist's approach to God, and, later on, his thought of
Sin and God's dealings with the erring sons of Adam.

d. *The Approach to God*

Such a God as has been described will receive man's worship. Worship is derived from the Anglo-Saxon *weorthan* and means "to ascribe worth." In this book of the *Praises of Israel* man ascribes worth to God:

> O come, let us worship and bow down;
> Let us kneel before the Lord, our Maker.
>
> (PSALM 95:6)

As might be expected this book is magnificently theocentric. God is the subject from first to last whether men sing the *Miserēre* or the *Hallel*. God is great and greatly to be praised is he. Great and marvelous are his works and when the singer thinks of these and recalls them to mind there is no limit to his praise and adoration. He ascribes worth to God in piled-up epithets:

> I will love thee, O Lord, my strength,
> O Lord, my fortress and my deliverer:
> My God, my rock, in whom I take refuge;
> My shield, my horn of salvation, my lofty
>   tower.
>
> (PSALM 18:1, 2)

The Hebrew poet does not usually multiply epithets in this fashion though the practice is common in psalms of Egypt and Babylon. But in those hymns from Babylon and Egypt one cannot escape the feeling that those epithets are intended to cozen and flatter the deity so that he may grant the worshiper's request which does not fail to conclude his hymn of praise. The praise is given to obtain something. In those alien psalms the worshiper ascribes worth to his god that he may magnify himself; his praise is not centered in God but is self-centered. With the Hebrew it is wholly otherwise. Requests and petitions are most exceptional in those hymns. The hymns of the Psalter are pure praise. The Hebrew sings because he must. He sings like the nightingale

that cannot but sing. Here are thoughts of sheer exultation
and worship untangled with any thought of self. Theology
here is fused into doxology.

> The Lord of heav'n confess,
> On high his glory raise.
> Him let all angels bless,
> Him all his armies praise.
> > Him glorify,
> > Sun, moon, and stars,
> > Ye higher spheres
> > And cloudy sky.
>
> From God your beings are,
> Him therefore famous make,
> You all created were
> When he the word but spake.
> > And from that place
> > Where fix'd you be
> > By his decree
> > You cannot pass.
>
> Praise God from earth below,
> Ye dragons and ye deeps;
> Fire, hail, clouds, wind, and snow,
> Whom in command he keeps.
> > Praise ye his name,
> > Hills great and small,
> > Trees low and tall,
> > Beasts wild and tame.
>
> All things that creep or fly,
> Ye kings, ye vulgar throng,
> All princes mean or high:
> Both men and virgins young
> > Ev'n young and old
> > Exalt his name,
> > For much his fame
> > Should be extoll'd.
>
> O let God's name be prais'd
> Above both earth and sky;
> For he his saints hath rais'd
> And set their horn on high:

> Ev'n those that be
> Of Isr'els race
> Near to his grace.
> The Lord praise ye
>
> (PSALM 148: Psalter in Metre)

"The Lord praise ye" is just the English translation of the Hebrew word "Hallelujah," with which this triumphant song of worship and adoration comes to its crashing close. That is what we mean by worship, the ascribing of worth, and nowhere outside the Hebrew Psalter do we find such songs of worship. The grandest Christian hymn, the *Te Deum Laudamus,* does not attain to this level for it combines worship with petition and is not magnificently objective like the psalm just quoted. In this matter of pure praise, ascribing of worth, we are all debtors to the Hebrew. None of our modern introverted anthropocentric hymnals has the strength of the Hebrew hymns with their theocentric extroverted emphasis. Modern churches might well make more use of this vehicle of praise. Apart from the hymn "Holy, holy, holy Lord God Almighty" there is very little in our hymnals that could approach this Hebrew level.

Nor need we imagine that those songs of praise rose from hearts that had not paused to think. With such a sublime God man must practice great caution in his approach. The great God must be approached in a fitting manner and men must be suitably prepared to enter into his presence. "Vessels meet for the Master's use" are required. For the Psalmist worship begins ere he crosses the threshold of the sanctuary. A searching of hearts must precede the entrance to the temple.

> Who shall ascend into the hill of the Lord?
> and who shall stand in his holy place?
> He that hath clean hands and a pure heart;
> who hath not lifted up his soul unto vanity,
> nor sworn deceitfully.
>
> (PSALM 24:3, 4)

The Hebrew laid great stress on the approach to God and the ritual may often seem to stress external matters but it did not neglect the more inward aspect. It is the pure in heart who shall see God:

> The Lord is righteous: he loveth righteousness;
> The upright shall behold his face.
>
> (PSALM 11:7)

Fools may rush in where angels fear to tread but the open vision is only for the purified:

> Search me, O God, and know my heart:
> try me, and know my thoughts;
> And see if *there be any* wicked way in me,
> and lead me in the way everlasting.
>
> (PSALM 139:23, 24)

Frequently we may see inscribed on the outside of our churches these words:

> Holiness becometh thine house, O Lord, for ever.
>
> (PSALM 93:5)

But it remains on the outside and never seems to affect the attitude of the worshiper. It was graven deep on the heart of the Hebrew and expressed in his worship.

> The Lord our God *is* a great God,
> and a great King above all gods.
>
> (PSALM 95:3)

> Honour and majesty *are* before him:
> strength and beauty *are* in his sanctuary.
> O worship the Lord in the beauty of holiness:
> fear before him all the earth.
>
> (PSALM 96:6, 9)

17

THE DIVINE REVELATION

We have already seen that the Bible does not argue about God: it assumes the existence of the divine being. God has made himself known to men in ways which they can understand. "His works declare him." The history of Israel has been the sphere in which men have seen his character disclosed. From his "acts" in their national history as from the works of his hands they have learned to know him as he is. Thus the two main channels of revelation are Nature and History and we proceed to consider these thoughts in the Psalter.

a. *In Nature*

Several psalms deal with Nature, and an examination of Psalms 8, 19:1–7, 29, 104, will show how the Hebrew felt in presence of this revelation. According to H. W. Robinson, "Nature is God's creation and constant activity, the direct and immediate expression of his power and will. That activity is transcendent, not immanent, Hebrew, not Greek." [1] The Hebrew could not view Nature apart from God: an attitude like that of the poet Wordsworth was im-

[1] *The Psalmists,* edited by D. C. Simpson, p. 50.

possible to the Hebrew. Indeed it may be questioned if the Hebrew would have recognised what we mean by Nature with the capital "N." But we may examine these songs and observe what the poet thought on this subject.

Psalm 29

The Psalmist deals with Nature both in its wilder and more peaceful aspects. But it is the former aspect that has most significance here. The terrifying aspects of Nature— and in the desert those aspects could be very terrifying—are here set forth, not to affright man and make him conscious of his weakness but rather to reveal the greatness of his God. It is significant of the Hebrew genius that Yahwe's wind is the east wind, the destroying, blasting, *Sherkiyeh,* that blows out of the desert. The poet sees here not the vast destruction wrought by the storm but rather the mighty power of the great God who controls and directs the storm.

The literary art of the poem is quite remarkable: the sevenfold repetition of the words "the voice of Yahwe" (*Qōl Yahwe*) gives the impression of successive thunder-claps. It is difficult to secure this effect in the English translation though the repetition of the words *Qōl Yahwe,* each word with a full accent, would help. Poets have frequently used such literary devices, as witness Byron's similar description of a thunderstorm:

> From peak to peak, the rattling crags among,
> Leaps the live thunder.
>
> (*Childe Harold*)

Byron has caught something of the feeling of the Hebrew bard, but Coleridge is less successful in his *Hymn in the Valley of Chamonix:*

> Motionless torrents! silent cataracts!
> Who made you glorious as the gates of heaven
> Beneath the keen full moon? Who bade the sun

Clothe you with rainbows? Who, with living
flowers
Of loveliest blue, spread garlands at your feet?
God! let the torrents, like a shout of nations,
Answer, and let the ice-plains echo, God!
God! sing ye meadow streams with gladsome
voice!
Ye pine-groves, with your soft and soul-like
sounds:
And they, too, have a voice, yon piles of snow,
And in their perilous fall shall thunder, God!

This artificial and self-conscious apostrophe compares
feebly with the rugged grandeur of the psalm. It is as if one
should set a polished stone beside the monoliths of Baalbek.

The psalm begins with a summons to praise addressed
to the heavenly court, but swiftly passes from heaven to
earth beneath, where the storm rages. The picture here may
be composite, for, with lapidary expressions, the poet moves
from the Mediterranean Sea—where such storms most frequently arise—to the heights of Lebanon and Hermon,
then south to the wilderness of Kadesh. There is nothing
here of "the ruffian billows" or "the rude imperious surge"
that filled the mind of Shakspere in presence of the storm.
The poet is not interested in the sea itself, but in Jehovah
who rouses it to fury and can tame it to subjection. Mountains reel and stagger while the lofty cedars are broken and
laid low before the sweeping tempest. With a strange combination of the humorous and the terrible, which is characteristic of the Hebrew, the poet sees those hills dancing like
a young ox and skipping like a calf. The poet seems to think
of the animals as sharing in his own wild joy as he stands
clapping his hands in presence of the vast destruction
wrought by the hurricane, while

In his temple everything says "Glory."

All that has transpired on earth is *ad gloriam Dei*. Earth

strewn with wreckage—and God glorified! In the calm and
peace of his own eternity Jehovah sits enthroned:

> The Lord sits above the flood,
> Sits the Lord, king for ever.

Most scholars regard verse 11 as a later addition to the
song but this is surely an error. In a literary sense the song
might end at verse 10, but the singer was thinking less of
literary fitness than of religious values and vital necessities.
It is, indeed, a great matter to know we have a great God
in whose hands such vast powers reside. It is a greater
matter, however, to know that such a God hears his people's
prayers and sets all his powers at the disposal of needy men.
Thus we would prefer to translate the last verse as a prayer
and render thus:

> May the Lord grant his people power!
> May the Lord bless his folk with peace!

And so, as Delitzsch points out, the song that began with
the *Gloria in excelsis* ends with *Pax in terra*.

Psalm 8

In this song we have a more peaceful atmosphere. It
may be called a night-piece, for there is no mention of the
sun. It is a comforting word because today human life
seems to suffer from a kind of astronomical intimidation.
Men are terrified by the stars and the thought of the vast
stellar interspaces. Has not the astronomer told us that he
has searched the skies and finds no need for the "God-
hypothesis"? We can understand the mood of Thomas Carlyle who stood under the starry sky and said, "It's a sair
sicht" (it is a sore sight). We have set Natural Law in the
place of God and substituted the fear of life for the fear of
the Lord: life is intimidated. The Psalmist did not feel thus
about the stars; they brought him comfort and blessing.
The stars spoke of the divine greatness: they revealed

God's majesty and power. They were the work of his fingers—and what fingerwork!—and the creation of his hands, God's handiwork.

> He calleth them all by name; by the greatness of
> his might, and for that he is strong in power, not
> one of them is lacking.   (ISAIAH 40:26)

It may be that the opening exclamation of adoration is provoked by the singer's overhearing little children sing, for here children mingle with the stars. What a potent deity is this who sets such power in little things and uses "things that are not that he might bring to nought things that are" (I Corinthians 1:28)! Little children that seemed so small and insignificant as not to count at all, a Moses in his ark of bulrushes, a Joseph with his childhood dreams, a Samuel with his little coat, a David with his boyhood sling, a Jesus wrapped in swaddling clothes and laid in a manger, all so little and small that it seems nothing could ever come of such things—it is all so wonderful and so passing strange. But God's thoughts are not our thoughts nor are his ways our ways. If God can do that with little things, how much more will he do when he arises in the greatness of his power. Thus the singer is comforted and marvelously helped as he thinks:

> Lo, these are but the outskirts of his ways:
> And how small a whisper do we hear of him.
> (JOB 26:14)

The half hath not been told. Thus we can understand the glowing enthusiasm in the heart of the singer and how nothing but a great burst of praise could open and close this song:

> O Jehovah, our Lord,
> How excellent is thy name in all the earth,
> Whose majesty is rehearsed above the heavens.

This rendering seems best and it entails no alteration in

the Hebrew text. The music of the spheres answers and sings responsively to the clear trebles of the children's choir. Earth's little song is gathered up to heaven's mighty harmonies, and the universe is filled with the great Creator's praise.

To the poet Nature is inconceivable without the divine background. He cannot see Nature without the simultaneous thought of God and Man. In this Tennyson and Burns most closely resemble the Hebrew bard. Nature to the Psalmist half conceals and half reveals God: it reveals enough to confirm man's faith and conceals enough to stimulate his reverence and quicken his devotion. For reverence is the fundamental quality of the Hebrew mind. "The fear of the Lord" is in his very bones, and the consciousness of the vast gulf that separates deity from humanity is present from beginning to end of Scripture. Here is the most fundamental thing in the Old Testament, and side by side with it is found an almost equally fundamental feeling of confidence and trust in the same God. Between those two poles of thought lies the whole of Hebrew piety. At times the one thought may be emphasised to the almost total exclusion of the other, and here we have one of those frequent tensions in Old Testament theology. But both thoughts are present to the same mind, and at times they are combined in striking fashion, as in the present psalm and again in Psalm 147:

> Those that are broken in their heart
> and grieved in their minds
> He healeth, and their painful wounds
> he tenderly upbinds.
> He counts the number of the stars:
> he names them ev'ry one.
> Great is our Lord and of great power,
> his wisdom search can none.
>
> (PSALM 147:3, 4)

"The melody of the psalm," says Weiser, "is woven together

out of fear of, and joy in, God." They are wrought together here as in a seamless garment, for the Hebrew could not make it otherwise.

Thus, on one side, we get a view of the apparent *insignificance of man.*

> What is man that thou art mindful of him,
> and the son of man that thou visitest him?

The word used for man in the first line (*Enosh*) signifies weak, creaturely man, while the word in the second line (*ben-Adam*) expresses his mortality and "earth-bornness." Because the singer is conscious of God's greatness and distance from all human frailty, this is his first thought. To the Hebrew it was impossible to explain man in naturalistic fashion: man could only be explained or interpreted with reference to God. Nor, be it added, could God be explained or interpreted save by reference to the highest man knew— his own consciousness. Here the singer magnifies his God by an apparent belittling of man, and such a thought may find ready acceptance with us who live in a machine age and have ceased to believe that man is made in the image of God but is constituted rather by a chemical formula. But that is precisely because we have lost the faculty of wonder and adoration. The atheism of fear has displaced the vital faith of our fathers and the discoveries of modern Science have produced a new generation of "quakers" who tremble at the work of their own hands. If man is insignificant as a worm or a maggot, something wholly insignificant in face of the vast stellar system, then there remains nothing for us but "to eat, drink, and be merry, for tomorrow we die." On this basis life itself has given us the knock-out blow and we are left with nothing but the sense of frustration and defeat.

But we can never rest there. The Psalmist has another thought, a second thought, and it is the thought of the *significance of man.* Man is made in the image of God and created for fellowship with him. He is a partner in the divine. The thought of the divine greatness is here crossed by the thought of the divine mercy (verses 5–8). Life becomes luminous with God. Here is the *Magna Charta* of humanity. The great God does not dwell in lonely greatness, but has assumed man to his fellowship and endowed him with prerogatives and powers not unlike his own. Man is set as "a little god" in the realm of Nature: he is God's vicegerent and is given lordship over all the lower creation. Man is the "child of a king" and "monarch of all he surveys" because the Lord hath set his pleasure upon him. Like Paul, in all pride and humility, he can say,

> By the grace of God I am what I am.
> (I CORINTHIANS 15:10)

In so saying he would express profound reverence before God and assert the dignity of man in the face of Nature. There is nothing here of the Greek *hybris* (daring, defiant presumption), no overweening self-confidence that will defy high heaven and steal the blessing for mankind. There is no Semitic Prometheus here. That is the path of pagan humanism and it leads to the glorification of man and man's endeavor. "Much that is mighty lives," says Sophocles,[2] "but nothing is mightier than man." That is the expression of a mood that runs from the tower of Babel to the present atomic age. Man is the measure of all things. That is an axiom familiar to us, but it was foreign to the Hebrew way of thinking. The Psalmist was saved from the final descent by the vision of human insignificance, and by his vision of human significance and worth as *something not self-attained but God-given*. Man's dominion is not won by some titanic Prometheus who steals fire from heaven: man's dominion is given by God and man becomes a fellow-worker with the God of grace. The tension of thought is resolved in

[2] *Antigone,* line 332.

experience and the final synthesis satisfies. The Greek idea issued in the region of aesthetic and Greek tragedy was its fruit: the Hebrew thought remained to fructify all truly creative culture through all the ages.

And so the poet returned finally to his starting point and his last word is as his first:

> O Jehovah, our Lord
> How excellent is thy name in all the earth.

Psalm 19:1–6

This psalm may well be compared with Psalm 8. Both songs reveal the sense of wonder in face of Nature that quickens man to reverence and adoration. The poet in Psalm 8 is more directly concerned with the relation between Creator and Creation, while the singer here dwells rather on the character of revelation. Without doubt the present singer is the greater poet: his speech is picturesque and forceful and his imaginative insight lifts him high above the poet of the earlier psalm. This can be clearly seen in the vitalising influence which he has exercised on Goethe, Haydn, and Beethoven. His music has moved those masters to lofty creative work in the realm of music. Our own Shakespeare may have had this psalm in mind when he wrote:

> Look how the floor of heaven
> Is thick inlaid with patines of bright gold;
> There's not the smallest orb which thou behold'st
> But in his motion like an angel sings,
> Still quiring to the young-eyed cherubims.
> Such harmony is in immortal souls;
> But whilst this muddy vesture of decay
> Doth grossly close it in, we cannot hear it.
> *(Merchant of Venice)*

To the Hebrew Nature is God's creation: there is no room here for such a vague pantheism as we find in Wordsworth:

> . . . a sense sublime
> Of something far more deeply interfused,
> Whose dwelling is the light of setting suns,
> And the round ocean and the living air,
> And the blue sky, and in the mind of man:
> A motion, and a spirit, that impels
> All thinking things, all objects of thought,
> And rolls through all things.
>
> (*Lines Written above Tintern Abbey*)

To the Hebrew, Nature is that which God created: it is his servant and minister. It is set and appointed to show forth his praise and to mediate the revelation of the divine. The opening lines of the song employ the literary figure of *Chiasmus* and the Hebrew order can best be preserved thus:

> The heavens are telling the glory of God,
>   And the work of his hands the firmament proclaims.

The revelation here given is not limited with the limitations of human speech which might confine it to one people or race. Its speech is understood to the ends of the earth. He who has ears unstopped to hear those celestial melodies, and eyes open to behold God in Nature, will not seek to resolve life into chemical formulae or physical equations, but will rather regard those formulae and equations as notes in the celestial symphony, in which the divine wisdom and power are made audible. Thus all science may become reverent and engage in the process of "thinking God's thoughts after him." The "music of the spheres" will provoke an answering song in the heart of man until his whole life becomes resonant and beautiful with praise.

The singer's attitude to Nature is emphasised by the ancient hymn to the sun (verses 4b–6) which the writer has taken over and embedded in his song. It has its roots in ancient mythology and its pagan origin is clearly seen. But monotheism is the death of mythology. When the Hebrew took over those alien elements he touched them with his

own genius till they ring like iron and shine like cloth of
gold. It was a current thought of antiquity that the sun-god,
after his long day's journey across the sky, descended to the
ocean bed, there to spend the night with his bride before
resuming his trek across the ocean floor to begin his journey
through the sky once more. It would seem as if a line has
dropped out here as the poetical structure reveals a lacuna.
The word, too, for *in them* may, by a very slight change, be
read *in the sea*, and the verse may be translated thus:

> For the sun he hath set a tent in the sea
>
> .   .   .   .   .   .
>
> Like a bridegroom he comes from his chamber
> And rejoices like a hero to run his course:
> His going forth is from the end of the heavens,
> And his circuit unto the ends of it;
> And nothing is hid from the heat thereof.

Here the original myth of the sun-god has faded to a poetic
simile, "like a bridegroom." The sun-god has disappeared
and is here only as a natural object in the service of the
great God who has appointed to him his daily duty. The
old pagan myth is interpreted in the light of Hebrew monotheism:

> Sun, moon, and stars, him glorify.
>
> (PSALM 148:3)

Psalm 104

Here we come to the longest of the Nature psalms, and
this song is full of beauty. Form and substance are alike
remarkable. Here we have a wealth of imaginative insight
and a depth of pathos that are rarely found in Hebrew literature. Only the book of Job or the poetry of Isaiah 40–55
may be compared with what we have here. In contrast with
Psalm 8, which is full of devout simplicity, and Psalm
19:1–6, which impresses by its antique and primitive cast,

Psalm 104 is almost modern in its range of sentiment. It is comprehensive and complete, ranging from earth to heaven and occupying the interspaces of air and sea, filled with loftiest adoration and animated by elevated feeling throughout. Its lyrical miniatures, too, are striking in their detailed beauty of description. Nothing seems to escape the eye of the poet: to him everything reveals the manifold wisdom of God.

Hymns of this kind, though not of the same quality, are not uncommon in all early literatures, both Oriental and Occidental. Only in Egypt, however, do we find anything comparable to the present poem. Scholars are agreed that Ikhnaton's *Hymn to the Sun-god,* which may be dated about 1370 B.C., has many ideas and expressions in common with this song, and it may have exercised a real influence upon the poet of this psalm. That such external influences did play a part in the formation of Hebrew literature is not to be denied, but such influences need not be over-estimated. All that the Hebrew borrowed he made his own and stamped it with his peculiar genius. That can be seen in his treatment of Babylonian myths in Genesis 1 and it can be seen here. The god of Ikhnaton was the sun, but, to the Hebrew, God was the creator of the sun. The Egyptian god was part and parcel of Nature, but the Hebrew Jehovah stands outside and above Nature. He rules over all. In these matters it is not the similarities that signify but the differences. The distinguishing features of Hebrew psalmody must not be overlooked.

The psalm opens with a summons to praise and it closes with the same. Within that framework of personal devotion the poem is set. Its theme is the greatness of God. Wherever the singer looks, in heaven above or earth beneath or out upon the sea, he finds food for wonder, praise and adoration. Here we have a sense of the *numinous* as in Isaiah 6, the

sense of God in all his might and kingly power, the great
God in whose hands all things stand and by whose power
they are sustained in being. For the religious value of this
psalm lies in its insight into the divine purpose of Creation.
The whole teleological argument is here in poetic form;
there is wisdom and purpose in all the manifold forms of
Nature. "In all his ways most wonderful" he has built this
universe. His works declare him.

And so there pervades the poem that characteristic feeling of optimism that pertains to all Hebrew literature.
Not that the writer failed to see the darker side of life which
we tend to emphasise with our talk about "Nature red in
tooth and claw," but he saw beyond that to God, and in the
light of that vision he knew the universe to be friendly. He
knows of Leviathan and the lions that roar and raven; he
knows of smoking volcanoes that belch forth death and ruin
for all, but he knows God and he is satisfied. Like the writer
in Genesis 1 he surveys the total scene and "behold, it is
very good." The poet is not ignorant of the fact of sin and its
ruinous effects that have marred God's fair handiwork. Thus
in the latter part (*verse* 31) the writer passes from the
aesthetic viewpoint to that of morality and religion
and finds that, ultimately, all is moral through and
through.

The poet's intention is to glorify God, for wisdom is
revealed in all his works. He not only marvels at the might
that made the universe, but adores the wisdom that has
related all things so purposefully. It is not only Creation but
the sustaining Providence that fills his mind with awe and
moves his heart to praise. Barnes has remarked that the
song might have been written by a Deist were it not for the
repeated mention of Jehovah. Here, indeed, we have the
farthest remove from the Deistic view, which holds God
made the world and left it to its own resources. To the

Psalmist here God is the living God, present in all his works, and ever working still with wisdom and purposeful intent. The springs in the valley are set there to water the beasts of the forest (*verses* 10, 11), else would they die of thirst. Among the shrubs the birds are singing, for God has made the desert scrub for them. We recall the words of Jesus:

> Are not two sparrows sold for a penny? And not one of them shall fall on the ground without your Father: but the very hairs of your head are all numbered.   (MATTHEW 10:29, 30)

The hills, too, that might wither for lack of water from the subterranean depths, God waters with rain from his heaven above (*verse* 13). All this God does because he is mindful of his creatures.

> He maketh grass to grow for cattle,
> and fodder for the animals that work for man
> to bring forth food from the earth;
> And wine that cheers man's heart,
> oil, to make his face shine,
> and bread that stays the heart of man.

So should we translate verses 14, 15. God thinks not only of bare sustenance: he has regard to man's joy and beauty. He cares not only for man's being, but for his well-being. The trees, so tall and spreading, which no man planted but Jehovah himself, those mighty cedars of Lebanon, they drink their fill and are satisfied. The birds, too, find a home in them and the cypress is appointed for the ostrich's abode (*verse* 17). Those scars and clefts on the hillside, what purpose do they serve?

> The high hills are for the wild goats
> and the rocks are a refuge for the badger.
>   (VERSE 16)

Creation is intelligent: it is shot through with purpose. In wisdom God made all these things.

The stars in their courses, the sun in its rise as in its setting, the moon in its seasons, all are appointed of God to minister to man's need and give order and proportion to his living. Night is for the beasts: while they prowl man sleeps, but in the daytime man will fare forth to his task. With delicate intuition the poet thinks of the lion's roar that terrifies man by night as they cry to God for food. God gives, and what he gives they gather. Everywhere the same divine wisdom is revealed. In *verses* 24–26 we have a strange figure which was not too strange for the Hebrew:

> There go the sea-monsters,
> Leviathan, whom thou didst make for sport.

The great sea-dragon of antiquity, big, huge, clumsy, is here regarded as the plaything of God, as if the Almighty found delight in its uncouth antics. This is the way the Hebrew thought at times—it may reveal his humor—but he thought this way because he knew that only Almighty God could play with such a fearsome thing. God created this monster and it ministers to his purpose. Nothing here moves with aimless feet.

All these things the singer sees and he wonders at the power that made them and continually sustains them in being. He centers on the divine Providence. "All eyes look to thee," says Ikhnaton. God is the great provider: so many mouths to feed, and none are sent away empty! All they have and all they are they owe to his providing. In the sunshine of his countenance they live, and all their being is in him. Their breath is but an emanation from God himself (*verse* 29) and when God recalls it they die. Death reigns in Nature, and Nature is always being renewed. There is coming and there is going but the earth for ever remains young. Death also is part of the divine purpose: it also is the gift of God. And so the last word of the poet is like his first:

> Bless the Lord, O my soul.

Nature, thus, is one of the channels in which the divine revelation flows. "In wonder all philosophy began," says Coleridge,[3] "in wonder it ends, and admiration fills up the interspace." Or to use the expression of Plato: "Iris is the daughter of Thaumas." [4] That is how the Hebrew felt about it. Nature is the garment of God that half conceals and half reveals the majesty of Jehovah. It reveals enough to persuade man to praise and devotion, and it conceals enough to stir his curiosity and move him to the higher effort. To the Hebrew the world was "full of such a number of things," and his God made them all. His plan and his purpose were made known through Creation: his works declare his character. Nature exists to reveal deity.

b. *In History*

If Nature spoke in those terms to the Hebrew it was not otherwise with History. Nature is more impersonal than history, and the testimony of Nature is often ambiguous. But the concrete acts of Israel's history formed the sphere of divine revelation, and it was there the Hebrew came to know his God by the things his God did. Here we have no abstract system of thought but concrete acts, redemptions and large deliverances and "righteous acts" (Judges 5:11), from which the nation read forth the character of its God. In that history they marked the divine footprints and came to know the way of the Lord. It is a purely empirical theology when the poet writes:

> With the merciful thou wilt show thyself merciful;
> With the upright man thou wilt show thyself upright;
> With the pure thou wilt show thyself pure;
> and with the froward thou will show thyself froward.
> (PSALM 18:25, 26)

The writer who penned these words may be "speaking to

[3] *Aids to Reflection*, p. 177.
[4] *Theaetetus*, 155D.

God as one gentleman to another," [5] but he had the sense that God was not static but dynamic and that he was dealing with the living God. All their history taught the Jews that truth. History was not merely a succession of events in time: it was something that had its origin in God and moved in obedience to his will. History had a goal and events in time were the unfolding of the divine purpose. History revealed God because it was seen as a process with its roots in eternity and its origin in the divine initiative. And that divine purpose was clear even in face of actions that might appear to defiantly negate it. Men might "regard not the work of the Lord, neither consider the operation of his hands" (Isaiah 5:12), but their folly would soon be made clear. Godless folk might scoff and say:

> Let him make speed, *and* hasten his work, that we may see it; and let the counsel of the Holy One of Israel draw nigh and come, that we may know it!
> (ISAIAH 5:19)

God is in control of history, and what he does not will shall not come to pass (Isaiah 7:7). But what God wills does come to pass: he fashioned it long ago (Isaiah 22:11). Nor can any presumptuous soul think to thwart the purpose of God; the Assyrian may speak like all great military colossi who bestride the earth and say:

> By the strength of my hand have I done it, and by my wisdom; for I am prudent: I have removed the bounds of the people, and have robbed their treasures, and I have put down the inhabitants like a valiant man: and my hand hath found as a nest the riches of the people: and as one gathereth eggs *that are* left, have I gathered all the earth; and there was none that moved the wing or opened the mouth or peeped.   (ISAIAH 10:13, 14)

History may be interpreted so in terms of space and time,

---

[5] MacDonald, D. B., *The Hebrew Literary Genius,* p. 26.

as the issue of the interplay of human motives. But to interpret history aright we need a third dimension: we may not leave out God.

> Shall the ax boast itself against him that heweth therewith? or shall the saw magnify itself against him that shaketh it? as if the rod should shake *itself* against them that lift it up, *or* as if the staff should lift up *itself as if it were* no wood.
>
> (ISAIAH 10:15)

In history man is confronted with God: history emerges from the dramatic interaction of time and eternity.

One is here reminded of the striking description of Victor Hugo as he looks back on Waterloo:

> Was it possible that Napoleon should win this battle? We answer, No. Why? Because of Wellington? Because of Blucher? No. Because of God.
>
> For Napoleon to be conqueror at Waterloo was not in the law of the nineteenth century. Another series of facts was preparing in which Napoleon had no place. The ill-will of events had long been announced.
>
> It was time that this vast man should fall. The excessive weight of this man in human destiny disturbed the equilibrium. . . . The moment had come for incorruptible supreme equity to look to it. Probably the principles and elements upon which regular gravitations in the moral order as well as in the material depend began to murmur. Reeking blood, overcrowded cemeteries, weeping mothers—these are formidable pleaders. When the earth is suffering from a surcharge, there are mysterious moanings from the deeps which the heavens hear. Napoleon had been impeached before the Infinite, and his fall was decreed. He vexed God.[6]

Victor Hugo is speaking with a Greek accent here, but he is expressing the Hebrew idea of history, that God is Lord

[6] Hugo, Victor, *Les Misérables* (Everyman Edition, Vol. I, pp. 317, 318).

of history and that he directs all things to a spiritual end. Pharaoh, Nebuchadrezzar, Napoleon, Hitler may vex God for a time but the ultimate decency of things will finally be asserted and all flesh shall see it together. "The earth is the Lord's and the fulness thereof; the world and they that dwell therein" (Psalm 24:1). He orders all things and

> Surely the wrath of man shall praise thee:
> the remainder of wrath shalt thou restrain.
>
> (PSALM 76:10)

The evil will that defiantly asserts its own egoistic interests is made to subserve and promote the divine will which overrules and controls it. History is thus seen as God's continuous act of Creation: God descends, as it were, on the vertical line to strike into the horizontal plane of history. Perhaps this view of history might best be expressed in the simple words of Joseph as he stands in the presence of his brethren:

> God sent me before you to preserve you a posterity in the earth, and to save your lives by a great deliverance.
>
> So now, *it was* not you *that* sent me hither, but God: and he hath made me a father to Pharaoh, and lord of all his house, and a ruler throughout all the land of Egypt.   (GENESIS 45:7, 8)

This is history written not in two dimensions, but in three, and it receives its fullest exposition in the New Testament when the Apostles unfold the spiritual meaning of the Cross of Christ:

> The God of Abraham, and of Isaac, and of Jacob, the God of our fathers, hath glorified his Son Jesus: whom ye delivered up, and denied him in the presence of Pilate, when he was determined to let *him* go, . . . and killed the Prince of life, whom God hath raised from the dead; whereof we are witnesses.   (ACTS 3:13–15)

That is the supreme explosive encounter of man with God,

the conflict of powers infernal and supernal, and it must be recorded in three-dimensional form.

The Psalter, as already indicated, contains almost no historical references, but the national background and this moral idea of history are there throughout. The national history was sacramental and revelatory for there God revealed himself as "a help in troubles proved full well" (Psalm 46:1). The knowledge men have of God and his character rests on this history:

> In Judah *is* God known
> his name *is* great in Israel:
> In Salem also is his tabernacle,
> and his dwelling place in Zion.
> There brake he the arrows of the bow,
> the shield, and the sword, and the battle.
>
> (PSALM 76:1–3)

Old mythological elements may be present in such descriptions, elements derived from early Creation stories—these may be due to alien influence—and these are employed to set forth the mighty deeds of Israel's God.

> Thou hast broken Rahab in pieces as one that is slain;
> thou hast scattered thine enemies with thy strong arm.
> The heavens are thine, the earth also is thine;
> *as for* the world and the fulness thereof, thou hast founded
> them.   (PSALM 89:10, 11)

These mythological features were later superseded by the use of Israel's sacred legends, especially those dealing with the Exodus:

> I am the Lord thy God
> which brought thee up out of the land of Egypt.
>
> (PSALM 81:10)
> For he hath brought forth his people with joy,
> and his chosen with gladness;
> And gave them the lands of the heathen;
> and they inherited the labour of the people;

> That they might observe his statutes,
> and keep his laws. Hallelujah.
>
> (PSALM 105:43–45)

Perhaps no psalm is more significant in this connection than
Psalm 44. The whole Hebrew philosophy of history and the
doctrine of Providence shines forth clearly:

> We have heard with our ears, O God,
> Our fathers have told us *what* work thou didst
> in their days, in the times of old.
> *How* thou didst drive out the heathen with thy hand
> and plantedst them:
> *how* thou didst afflict the people and cast them out.
> For they got not the land in possession by their own
> sword,
> neither did their own arm save them;
> but thy right hand and thine arm, and the light of
> thy countenance,
> because thou hadst a favour unto them.
> Thou art my king, O God, command deliverances for
> Jacob.
> Through thee will we push down our enemies:
> through thy name will we tread them under that rise
> up against us.   (PSALM 44:1–5)

Psalms 105, 106 give a complete review of the national
history, beginning, as they do, with the words *Praise ye*
(*Hōdū*) and ending with *Hallelujah*. In that story of the
national life the singer saw revealed all the attributes of
God, his holiness, justice, goodness, truth. To him all history is moral through and through.

> There's a divinity that shapes our ends,
> Rough-hew them how we will.
>
> (SHAKESPERE, *Hamlet*)

That is how Shakespere expressed it, but the Hebrew poet
was more concrete and definite:

> Sits the Lord above the flood,
> Sits the Lord, king for ever.
>
> (PSALM 29:10)

At the center of things sits One who is holy, just, and true, the Covenant God of Israel. The pillars of his throne are truth and righteousness.

Nor did the Hebrew doubt the leading of God when sore stripes were laid upon his back:

> Therefore was the wrath of the Lord kindled against his people, insomuch that he abhorred his own inheritance.
> And he gave them into the hand of the heathen; and they that hated them ruled over them.
> Their enemies also oppressed them. . . . but they provoked him with their counsel, and were brought low for their iniquity.
>
> (PSALM 106:40–43)

Sometimes the poet will look at it from another angle and say:

Also to thee, O Lord, belongeth loving-kindness (*Chesed*),
For thou renderest to every man according to his work.

(PSALM 62:12)

Or yet again the Psalmist will say, and, in so saying, assert the dynamic quality of the divine righteousness:

> He gave them their request
> but sent leanness into their soul.
>
> (PSALM 106:15)

This profound moral conception of history is something unique, and we owe it to the Hebrews. Doubtless it was not always maintained on the highest level. It could, and did, issue into the pragmatic scheme of reward and punishment which we find in the book of Deuteronomy in particular and the Old Testament in general. The significance of this we will see later in our consideration of the doctrine of recompense and retribution. But this conception of history which we find among the Hebrews gave meaning to the sequence of world events and bestowed significance upon the life of the individual.

18

RELIGION IN LIFE

The Psalter deals with life, human life, and it considers it in the light of the eternal. The first psalm may have been written last of all as a general introduction to the complete Psalter. An introduction should tell us what the book is about. And so it does. Like the prologue to John's Gospel or the opening words of Ecclesiastes or like the overture to an opera, it sets forth the recurring *motifs* and highlights the theme. In this introductory song we observe the main marks of the Hebrew genius, concreteness and intensity. It is a song on *the Two Ways* and immediately we observe the Hebrew conception of religion: religion is a way of life. *It is walk, not talk.* Religion is revealed in action: it is a matter of walking, standing, sitting. And the Hebrew intensity is made clear in the thought that there are only two ways, and these ways are mutually exclusive. There is no middle path.

It is this aspect of the Hebrew genius we dislike. For the Hebrew will say "Either . . . or," where we want to say "Both . . . and." The Hebrew knows black and he knows white but he has no place for neutral grey. Compromise is foreign to his thought. It must be Jehovah or Baal, life or death, light or darkness. Jesus is thoroughly Hebrew when

he says, "Ye cannot serve God and Mammon." That Hebrew intensity cuts across all our selfishness and makes
short work of our innate tendency to base compromise. For
life begins, as Carlyle said, with *Entsagen,* renunciation.
The good life renounces some things and it is that renunciation that makes it the good life. Light has no fellowship
with darkness. A man is known by the kind of company he
does *not* keep. There are some persons whose society we
must forsake if we would walk in fellowship with God.

We would prefer to translate the second verse of the
introductory song thus:

> His delight is in the fear of the Lord,
> And in his law doth he meditate day and night.

The "fear of the Lord" is one of the Hebrew words for religion—the word *religion* does not occur in the Old Testament and is found only once in the New Testament—and
the *Law* here refers to this man's Bible. Probably that Bible
included no more than Deuteronomy, but he loved it. He
pored over it day and night, brooded upon it, kept humming
its words under his breath—such is the meaning of the
Hebrew word *meditate.* The good man loves his Bible: "The
best of books was in his hand," says John Bunyan, and its
words were music to his soul. It was "a lamp to his feet and
a light to his path." How men loved that Bible may be felt
and seen in the lyric tones of Psalm 19:7–11, or in the longest of all the psalms (119) which extols the purity, the
preciousness, and illuminating power of God's word. The
seeming monotony of that long psalm is relieved and illumined by the deep affection of the poet as he seems to find
words inadequate to bear the weight of his thankfulness for
the Bible:

> O how I love thy law!
> It is my meditation all the day.
>
> (PSALM 119:97)

In that far-off time the Bible was securely set in the affections of the good man.

For the Bible was the record of the divine revelation, and it gave man a full understanding of God and his purpose. It made clear the principles that lie behind the government of God's universe. These are moral principles, fundamental and foundational. The good life will endure: the wicked shall come to nought. The soul of the universe is just and "because God is God no work of man which is the expression of His will can come to nought." [1]

The Old Testament saint is here anticipating the Gospel: "a good tree cannot bring forth evil fruit" (Matthew 7:18). There is here the deliberate statement of the outworking of moral principles and the permanence of spiritual realities. Evil does not pay. Evil belongs to the realm of unreal things. Goodness, on the other hand, is real and substantial: it abides like the rich grain after threshing while the chaff is blown away. When God makes the final audit—and that surely is what the last verse means—the one will be absent and the other present. Good belongs to the realm of being: evil belongs to the realm of not-being. In the long run good is permanent, evil is transient.

Thus, right at the beginning, we have the Psalmist's *Credo,* his statement of things most surely believed. Faith and obedience are the guiding principles of his life, faith in a God who has revealed his will, in obedience to which the singer finds lasting joy. "In thy service is perfect freedom," and "in thy will is our peace."

The Psalmist leaves us in no doubt as to his religion. And he leaves us in no doubt as to the world in which he lived.

This was not the only way of life: all did not think as this singer. Over against the godly man who loved his Bible stood the ungodly who loved the world and the things of

[1] Weiser, Artur, *Die Psalmen,* p. 22.

the world. This division and distinction runs throughout the Psalter: these groups stand out as clear and distinct as our modern political parties or our ecclesiastical sects. The *Saints* (*Chasidim*) or godly ones, the *Righteous* (*Tsaddiqim*), the *Poor* (*Ebyonim*), the *Humble Ones* ('*Anavim*, '*Aniyyim*), stand over against the *Wicked* (*Resha'im*) and the *Sinners* (*Chatta'im*). This juxtaposition of parties and groups might suggest that the term *righteous* is used here merely in a relative sense. From this viewpoint certain expressions in the Psalter may seem less offensive to us, for the attitude of Pharisaism is not in favor with us and we dislike all righteousness that takes its stand on works alone.

The Psalter, and the Old Testament generally, are convinced of the universality of sin and know well that in any absolute sense "there is none righteous, no, not one." But the term "righteous" is applied in the Old Testament to various figures like Enoch, Noah, Daniel, Job (Genesis 6:9, 7:1; Ezekiel 14:14, 20). The term is not applied directly to Abraham or Moses, and no such thing as sinlessness is predicated of any Old Testament character. In later usage the element of comparison is generally present or implied. In the book of Habakkuk (1:13) the Jews are referred to as righteous in comparison with their oppressors, the Chaldeans.

After the Exile the term seems to acquire a more precise connotation and denotes those Jews who were faithful to God and kept the Law in comparison with those renegade Jews who were willing to barter their spiritual heritage for a mess of political pottage and were ready to accommodate themselves to the emerging social and political circumstances of their times. The righteous were those who tried to maintain the faith of their fathers in its pristine purity and who rejected all compromises and innovations. The conflict may have been one between liberals and conservatives in politics and Fundamentalists and Modernists in religion. The Righteous may have been unduly narrow and bigoted, and the Wicked may have been a little too latitudinarian but we may well believe the faults were not all on one side. Genuine zeal might run to intolerance on the side of the Righteous, while broadmindedness might issue in brutality and oppression on the part of the Wicked. We have only the psalms of the Righteous in the Psalter and it might have been interesting to see what the profane rascals had to say for themselves. We should bear in mind that they were not allowed to speak for themselves: the Saints saw to it that their testimony was stilled.

The writer here is not engaged in the act of blackballing the Saints and whitewashing the Sinners. The conflict may have been not unlike that between Orthodox and Reform Judaism, or that between various Christian denominations and sects. But this must be kept in view as we look at religion in life in that far-off time.

Quite clearly there were elements of danger in this idea of righteousness, and while Pharisaism does not appear prominently in the Psalter—for the Psalter centers on God, not man—we can discern clearly the first faint outlines of the unlovely thing that we know as Pharisaism in the Gospels. To quote the words of H. W. Robinson:

> "The inner life of religion is so subtle and delicate, that when moral conditions are emphasised prominence may be given to man rather than God, and moral respectability may replace the life-breath of faith.[2]

Thus we come finally to the Pharisee who stood in all his pride beside the publican and said: "God, I thank thee that I am not as other men" (Luke 18:11).

There are some psalms (5, 7, 17, 26) which strongly assert

---

[2] *The Psalmists*, edited by D. C. Simpson, p. 54.

man's innocence and do so before God in such fashion that we cannot escape the impression that we are in the presence of something very like "righteousness by works."

> Judge me, O Lord,
> For I have walked in mine integrity;
> I have trusted also in the Lord without wavering.
> (PSALM 26:1)

That may seem a bold word to us: it occurs again in Psalm 7:8. In Psalm 18 David may still be speaking to God "as one gentleman to another" (D. B. MacDonald) when he says:

> I was also upright before him,
> and I kept myself from mine iniquity.
> (PSALM 18:23)

That would certainly not be the language of Christian prayer. Nor would the words of Psalm 101 be our words:

> I will behave myself wisely in a perfect way . . .
> I will walk within my house with a perfect heart.
> (VERSE 2)

Psalm 44 is a *Community Lament* and it shows the group could take this same attitude:

> All this is come upon us: yet have we not forgotten thee,
> Neither have we dealt falsely in thy covenant.
> Our heart is not turned back,
> Neither have our steps declined from thy way.
> (PSALM 44:17, 18)

But such voices are the exception in the Psalter. The main emphasis is upon God and his mighty works. Where such voices are heard we may take it that the covenant idea is being interpreted in a narrow legalistic way. For the term *covenant* is inadequate to express the real nature of God's dealings with his people: the secular associations of that term led frequently to an obscuring of the aspect of grace.[3] Wherever the influence of the great prophets and Deuteronomy had come it emphasised the aspect of wondrous love

[3] Köhler, L., *Theologie des Alten Testaments*, p. 46.

and grace. That is the prevailing mood of the Psalter. Later
Judaism became wholly legalistic and religion was construed
in terms of *quid pro quo*, wherein the idea of mutual obligation and mutual service supplants the idea of free and undeserved grace. That which began in the Psalter and gained
momentum in later Judaism is seen in its final form in the
pages of the New Testament. But between the first psalm,
which may have been written last of all, and the Pharisee
of the New Testament there is a great gulf fixed.

Thus an attitude of humility will best become the godly
man. "Nothing in my hand I bring."

> Who can discern his errors?
> Cleanse thou me from hidden faults:
> Keep back thy servant also from presumptu-
>   ous sins;
> Let them not have dominion over me.
>   (PSALM 19:12, 13)

Like the religion of the New Testament the religion of the
Psalter begins with *the Given*. All true religion begins so.
Its foundation is not in something man does or has done: its
basis is in God and in what God has done, what God has
given. This may seem almost a commonplace but it needs
to be emphasised, for this is not how we usually think of
religion. It is significant of the time in which we live that
the words most frequently recurring in our religious teaching are words like self-conquest, aspiration, attainment,
self-realisation, and so on. These words reflect the modern
viewpoint: they are aggressive words that flatter the human
ego and center on human endeavor. They are the expression of a belief that man is the measure of all things. It is
not so in the New Testament. Jesus does not say to men,
"Come unto me all ye who have the will to power and I
will make you supermen." Nor does he say, "Ye shall be
wise as God": that is not the voice of God. It is the word
of the serpent. What Jesus says is, "Come unto me all ye

that labor and are heavy-laden and I will give you rest."
And John sets forth the central truth of religion in John
3:16:

> God so loved the world that he gave his only-
> begotten son that whosoever believeth in him
> should not perish but have life everlasting.

Nor is it otherwise with the Psalms. Here religion begins
with something that God has done:

> I waited patiently for the Lord;
> And he inclined to me, and heard my cry.
>
> He brought me up also out of an horrible pit,
>   out of the miry clay,
> And set my feet upon a rock, *and* established
>   my goings.
>
> And he put a new song in my mouth, even
> praise unto our God:
> Many shall see *it,* and fear,
> And shall trust in the Lord.

(PSALM 40:1-3)

These verses tell of the wonderful thing God has done. The
details of his piteous plight are barely mentioned as the
poet hastens to set forth the saving activity of God. What
a story he might have told of himself and his suffering, but
all his song is of the Lord who redeemed him. With typical
Hebrew reverence and reticence all that concerns the *ego*
is lost to view in the vision of the divine mercy. All is
of God, all he is and all he hopes to be. The pit and the
clay are distant memories while the rock on which he stands
and his firm going are vital experience. The very words in
which he speaks of this, the song itself, are the gift of God.
Gunkel suggests that this surprising experience of grace
made the man a poet, but there is something deeper here.
The poet feels that the new view of the world, and the new
attitudes to life thereby attained, can find expression only
in a new song, the song of the redeemed. Did not Frank T.

Bullen tell us that on the day after his conversion as he crossed Boston Common all the birds seemed to be singing a new song?

> Birds with gladder songs o'erflow,
> Flowers with richer beauties shine,
> Whilst I know, as now I know,
> I am His, and He is mine.

If any man be in Christ, says Paul, he is a new creature. That is precisely what the Psalmist felt, and, as he will go on to say, frail mortal speech is unable to bear the weight of gratitude that burdens the man who has known what he has known. The wonderful 103rd Psalm throbs and glows with the passion of the redeemed, with the joy of a heart that feels its endless obligation to God:

> Bless the Lord, O my soul;
> And all that is within me, *bless* his holy
>   name. . . .
> Who forgiveth all thine iniquities;
> Who healeth all thy diseases;
> Who redeemeth thy life from destruction;
> Who crowneth thee with loving-kindness and
>   and tender mercies;
> Who satisfieth thy mouth with good *things;*
> *So that* thy youth is renewed like the eagle's
>   (VERSES 1–5)

"Like as a father pitieth his children" (verse 13): here is the first to glimpse the meaning of that mighty word—*Father*. Doubtless the Psalmist did not understand that word as Jesus did: there were limitations in the early view that must abide until the Lord of glory shall remove them by the complete unveiling of the intention of the divine heart. But, even with his partial insight, the ancient singer has seen, however dimly, that God is love, the repetition of the words "them that fear him" (verses 11, 17) conveys the sense of holy awe that fills the mind of the poet in presence of this revelation. Holy awe and exulting love fill the heart as he looks on the wondrous thing God has wrought (verses 14–18).

That this consciousness may belong to the group as to the individual is seen from a psalm like 48. Here we have a group of pilgrims making procession round the city (verses 12–14). History here becomes meaningful and reve-latory. Every holy association and every sacred memory are passed in review. Here they behold the tower built by David, Israel's darling king, and over there is the rampart that his heroes stormed to make the city his, when first they took it from the Jebusites. And there, again, down there, just below this tower, stood that insolent herald of Sen-nacherib who defied the God of Israel and whose words struck terror to the heart of Hezekiah. On that very wall walked Isaiah with all his wondrous eloquence and his amaz-ing faith. For Isaiah knew, as the Psalmist knew, that Israel's help came from "the Lord who made heaven and earth." Was there ever such a city as this? Here it was they took Jeremiah when he sought to go forth, and up there, too, is the room where the ruthless king Jehoiakim sat by the fire and slit the prophet's writing to pieces and little thought that the pen would prove mightier than the pen-knife (Jeremiah 36). Memories and memories! Every nook and corner of that city is soaked and permeated with his-tory and grace, with judgment and mercy. It all rises before them as they process round these walls.

> Walk about Zion, circling her,
>   count her towers:
> Give heed to her bulwarks,
>   consider her palaces:
> That ye may tell to later generations
>   "Such is God,"
> Our God, for ever and ever!
>   He will be our guide.
>
> (PSALM 48:12–14)

The great fact of religion is man's infinite need and God's boundless power and grace. It begins with something God has done.

> They that trust in the Lord
> *Shall be* as Mount Zion which cannot be moved
>   but abideth for ever.
> *As* the mountains *are* round about Jerusalem
> So the Lord is round about his people
> From henceforth even for ever.
>
> (PSALM 125:1, 2)

On the basis of this faith man is moved to high and noble endeavor. Religion articulates itself in thought, attitude, and action. Psalm 11 presents the picture of an old-time Mr. Greatheart who proclaims and asserts faith in face of faint-hearted friends. Against all such counsels of expediency the good man maintains vital faith in God. "Flee like a bird to the mountain" (Psalm 11:1) finds its true response in the word of Nehemiah, "Should such a man as I flee?" (Nehemiah 6:11). Faith is twin sister to courage but the "fearful and unbelieving" belong together (Revelation 21:8). Base prudential maxims find no place in the Christian life. It is noteworthy that when Paul wrote of the Christian armor he described a girdle for the loins, a helmet for the head, a breastplate, a sword, a shield, but never a piece for man's back (Ephesians 6:14). Plainly Paul did not contemplate the possibility of a man running away in the strife of life. Monasticism, Stoicism, and asceticism might adopt this attitude but it was foreign to Christianity as we understand it. It was foreign to the life of faith as the Psalmist understood it. His heart is fixed, trusting in the Lord.

For faith emphasises the uplook rather than the outlook. So often this is strikingly presented in these songs. We see princes gathered together and hosts arrayed against the Lord and his Anointed (Psalm 2). Suddenly the singer lifts

his eyes above the troubled angry world and sees the Lord
sitting in the calm and peace of his own eternity.

> He that sitteth in the heavens shall laugh:
> The Lord shall have them in derision.
>
> (PSALM 2:4)

In Psalm 36 the poet opens with a woeful picture of human
wickedness that might well chill the heart of the faithful.
In verse 5 the scene changes with an abruptness that has
puzzled most commentators. There is no difficulty here: the
poet is "thinking with the eye," and his eye had passed
from the outlook to the uplook. In these cases the English
translation does not do justice to the original. In verse 5
the first word is *Yahwe,* and it is an exclamation:

> O Lord! thy loving-kindness is in the heavens;
> Thy faithfulness reaches unto the skies.

The Lord is on his throne and the pillars of that throne are
truth and righteousness. Such faith empowers and gives
irresistible might. The fear of the Lord delivers from all
other fears. It blows grit into men and makes them *Great-
hearts.* Perhaps the word in Isaiah 28:16, "he that believeth
shall not make haste" might be better translated, "he that
believeth does not flee." Prophet and poet are of one mind
here. Faith and courage belong together and Psalm 11
shows them in triumphant action.

The Psalter is not unconscious of the tensions and stresses
that come in the life of faith. Weiser speaks of the "faith
that possesses" and the "faith that perseveres." The 23rd
Psalm may well represent the former: it is a typical *Psalm
of Trust.* But sometimes faith is not allowed to rest beside
still waters. It is beset and assailed by hostile circumstances
and it marks how far short of the divine intention are the
realities of life. Then impatiently it will cry, "How long,
O Lord, how long?" (Psalm 6:3, 90:13), or it may become
wholly interrogative and cry in distress, "My God, my God,

why?" (Psalm 22:1). But it is faith that speaks in all these forms: the tension is inherent in vital faith itself, and it becomes apparent according as the human or divine aspects of reality are emphasised. It is the same tension that we find expressed in the Gospel word: "Lord, I believe, help thou mine unbelief" (Mark 9:24), or again, "Blessed are they who have not seen and yet have believed" (John 20:29). Confronted by such contradictions that seem to threaten to annihilate faith, man's confidence in God is put to the test and faith fights for its very life. Faith is purchased at great cost. There is a real perseverance of the saints.

Psalm 42, which is an *Individual Lament,* and Psalm 124, which is a *Song of National Thanksgiving,* reveal this same strain and testify to the cost of faith:

> Why art thou cast down, O my soul?
> and why art thou disquieted within me?
> Hope thou in God, for I shall yet praise him,
> *who is* the health of my countenance and my
> God.
>
> (PSALM 42:5)

The interrupted communion will once more emerge into the clear light of day. God does not forsake his people. That was the Hebrew faith, and that faith is the secret of their survival. They believed in a God who was big enough to make the world and all therein, and they believed in a God good enough to make spiritual principles regulatory of his world.

Faith, too, will give its testimony and issue in service. The poet will proclaim the wondrous things God hath done. Righteousness, faithfulness, loving-kindness, truth—these are not epithets or attributes on which we may discourse and philosophise: they are the dynamic aspects of salvation and attest the God of grace (Psalm 32:11).

We have spoken of traces of Pharisaism in the Psalms but we should not overlook the fact that there is present also a deep sense of the reality of communion with God. The spiritual perception of the Psalmist comes at times no whit behind that of the New Testament saints. He may begin here with Psalm 16:

> I said to the Lord, thou art my Lord,
> All my welfare hangs on thee.
>
> (PSALM 16:2)

There is good MS authority for this translation and it seems to reflect the original. It is probable that by the time of this psalm philosophical ideas had infiltrated into Palestine and that the poet was familiar with them. If that be so he is giving a peculiar turn to the thought and, unlike the Greek, who thought of God as the highest in a series of goods, he speaks of God as *the only and all-inclusive good.* The man who possesses God possesses all. "All things are yours in Christ." This is in direct line with the teaching of the prophets, who taught that man's relation to God is a relation that affects every aspect of life and brings satisfaction full and complete (Psalm 73:25, 26). In him we live and move and have our being, and apart from him life is not worthy the name. Gunkel cites a prayer from Johannes Hertel's *indische Märchen* (p. 198) which reflects this same feeling of mystic communion:

> Thou only, O God, shalt dwell in my heart:
> Then what other need have I?

God is the *summum bonum,* and there is nothing on earth we desire beside him. This is the feeling of Psalm 63:1, 8:

> O God thou art my God: early will I seek thee:
> My soul thirsteth for thee, my flesh longeth
>   for thee. . . .
> My soul followeth hard after thee:
> Thy right hand upholdeth me.

More passionate is the expression in Psalm 42:2. Indeed this expression seemed too passionate to Jerome, who translated it:

> As the garden is made ready for irrigating
>   waters,
> So is my soul made ready for thee, O God.

Something less artificial and more ardent is here and we may render it thus:

> As pants the hind for waterbrooks
> So pants my soul for thee, O God.
> My soul doth thirst for God, the living God.
> When shall I come and behold the face of
>   God?

To appear before God or behold the face of God is the Hebrew expression for communion with God. The measure of the singer's grief at the absence of such communion may be measured by the glowing speech of Psalm 84 where men have come from afar to "behold the face of God":

> How lovely are thy dwelling-places
>   O Lord of hosts!
> With ardent longing my soul was spent
>   for the courts of the Lord;
> My heart and flesh now shout for joy
>   before the living God.
>
> (PSALM 84:1, 2)

Hope deferred made the heart of the earlier singer sick, but desire realised here constrains the worshiper to praise. His is the deep joy of one who has attained.

> Thus all things seek for rest,
> A home above, a home beneath the sod:
> The sun will seek the west,
> The bird will seek its nest,
> The heart another breast
> Whereon to lean: the spirit seeks its God.
>
> (DORA GREENWELL)

"Thou hast made us for thyself," says Augustine, "and our unquiet heart knows no rest till it finds rest in thee." God made man so. In this communion *the far God* and *the near God* become one and such distinctions as transcendence and immanence are resolved in vital religious experience.

One of the deepest words on this matter is spoken by the poet of Psalm 25:14:

> The secret of the Lord is with them that fear
> him, and he will show them his covenant.

The Hebrew words here are significant. *Secret* (*sodh*) here means "circle of familiar friends," whence it comes to mean intimacy, communion. It is the word used by Amos in 3:2 of his book:

> Surely the Lord God will do nothing without
> revealing his secret (*sodh*) unto his servants
> the prophets.

Jehovah has his circle of intimates, "those whom he whispers in the ear." Jeremiah knew that secret well and Hosea was no stranger to it, and Moses, too, with whom God "spake face to face," was of that inner circle. In the day of trouble a man could seek unto God:

> For in the time of trouble he shall hide me in
> his pavilion,
> In the secret of his tabernacle shall he hide me.
>
> (PSALM 27:5)

The life of communion is the safeguarded life. And even when the clouds are heavy with darkening storm a man will turn here for refuge (Psalm 13:1, 2).

This sense of communion is present most of all in Psalm 139. This is obviously a late psalm, for the loftiest religious ideas of religion are set forth in a most debased form of Hebrew. Here the personal note is struck from the beginning. *I* and *thou* confront each other in intimate personal communion. There is here a tremendous and overwhelming awareness of God, such as we find in Isaiah 6 or the Confessions of Jeremiah. Here the poet has come by an experience that is to him incomprehensible, yet as real as his own being. Awe and joy are mingled here, but joy is uppermost in the opening exclamation:

O Lord, thou hast searched me and known me.

Here surely is the *fons et origo* of all real religious experience. Here is an internalising and appropriating of the creed:

Hear, O Israel, the Lord thy God is one
(DEUTERONOMY 6:4).

Monotheism as an idea or system of thought may not touch us intimately: it may not come home to our bosoms as a personal thing. But, when we think of what is really implied, we cannot speak otherwise than does this poet here. "No man can say Jesus is Lord but in the Holy Spirit" (I Corinthians 12:3). How did the poet get this insight? It came partly through the teaching of Isaiah 40-66 but still more did it come through direct communion between the poet and his God. Thus the poet speaks by the spirit: the spirit that inspired the prophet inspired the poet. Before the surpassing revelation that comes to him in this communion he is "lost in wonder, love, and praise." There is a deep feeling of awe which, in the case of sinful men, might induce terror but in the case of the good man causes him to rejoice that all life "is under the eyes and by the blessing of God." Such knowledge could hamper and oppress, but it could also brace and comfort. Life is here immersed in God, and God is so great, so wonderful. The poet lives and moves and has his being in God. No movement of his is too small to pass unnoticed in heaven: his downsitting and uprising,—"our course and our camp" (J. M. P. Smith)—every item of the daily living God knows altogether. With all our ways he is acquainted: he knows our thoughts before they find expression in words, and there is nothing hid from the eyes of him with whom we have to deal. Other persons, all persons whom we know, must stand behind us or before us, but God envelops us all around. The mind of man might reel before such a thought, for it might rest upon us as a sheer nightmare cramping all activity. Or, again, it might liberate all our powers and urge us to highest endeavor. Such knowledge may pass the comprehension of mortal men, but the poet is certain that he is the object of such knowledge and he stands in amazement and adoration before the wondrous reality (verse 6).

This deep sense of the spiritual nature of God and of real fellowship with him led to a new attitude in regard to sacrifice. The sacrificial system in Israel constituted a very large part of popular religion, but much of that system seems to be of pagan origin. The prophets are unsparing in their denunciation of this system (Amos 5:23f., Isaiah 1:11f.) and to their teaching we can trace a new attitude in the Psalter, the attitude that deprecates material sacrifice and seeks to spiritualise the offerings. Some have held that this attitude is due to aesthetic considerations, as if the Jew tired of the sight of the unsightly mess that must have accompanied the sacrifice of bulls and goats. That does not seem at all probable. The whole context of the Psalmist's words on this matter points to its rejection in the light of a perception of God's real character and the demand for a spiritual worship. God is spirit and they that worship him must worship in spirit and in truth (John 4:24).

> Sacrifice and offering thou didst not desire:
> Burnt-offering and sin-offering hast thou not
> required.
>
> (PSALM 40:6)

The singer knew, as the prophets knew, that the fundamental relation between God and man is ethical and personal, not mechanical and material. Men had sensed that as early as the days of Samuel when a certain confusion was already entering into men's thoughts on religion: .

> Behold to obey is better than sacrifice,
> and to hearken than the fat of rams.
>
> (I SAMUEL 15:22)

Psalm 51: 16, 17 amplifies this statement in more positive fashion:

> For thou takest no pleasure in sacrifice:
> In proffered burnt-offering thou hast no delight.
> The sacrifices of God are a broken spirit—
> And a contrite heart, O God, thou wilt not despise.

The ethic of the clean heart cannot be substituted by the ethic of the thing done. Perhaps the words in Psalm 19:14 are replacing the formula that was usually employed in case of material sacrifice: the same change is found in Psalm 141:2:

> Let the words of my mouth and my heart's meditation
> Be acceptable in thy sight,
> O Lord, my rock and my redeemer.
>
> (PSALM 19:14)
>
> Let my prayer be set forth as incense before thee;
> The lifting up of my hands as the evening sacrifice.   (PSALM 141:2)

This is not the main thought of the Psalter, but it shows how choice spirits were feeling and thinking. For those choice spirits who communed deeply with God the material form of sacrifice was transcended and left behind: sacrifice had become spiritual.

The Old Testament is not the New Testament and there are elements in the Psalter that will seem to us decidedly sub-Christian. The singer's attitude to his enemies is not

Christian. Sometimes it is very far from being Christian. There is wrath here and hot indignation, and it is not holy wrath. But it is the opposite of moral languor. It springs from a passion for righteousness. Their anger is the natural reaction of those who love God and the good life against all that obstructs that higher purpose, but at times the expression of that wrath must offend the Christian conscience. The Psalmist had not learned to distinguish the sinner from his sin. We recoil from such an expression as that in Psalm 58:10:

> The righteous shall rejoice when he seeth the
> vengeance:
> He shall wash his feet in the blood of the
> wicked.

One almost shudders at such an outburst as we find in Psalm 137:8, 9:

> O daughter of Babylon, who art to be de-
> stroyed;
> happy *shall he be* that rewardeth thee as thou
> hast served us.
> Happy *shall he be,* that taketh and dasheth
> thy little ones against the stones.

No excuse can be made for such ferocity, but we should bear in mind the age-long suffering of the Jew. When a nation has endured a famine of justice it may bring on a delirium of conscience that will see red and speak red. These words are an index of national feeling. "But it shall not be so among you." "Vengeance is mine, I will repay, saith the Lord." But often the Jew had to cry, "How long, O Lord, how long?"

But not infrequently we can see a passion for righteousness motivating such expressions:

> Fill their faces with shame,
> That they may seek thy name, O Lord.
>
> > (PSALM 83:16)
>
> Do not I hate them, O Lord, that hate thee?

> And am not I grieved with those that rise up
>   against thee?
> I hate them with perfect hatred,
> I count them mine enemies.
>
> (PSALM 139:21, 22)

This repulsion of evil (cp. Psalm 7:9, 59:13) is the reverse side of the poet's zeal for truth and righteousness. He despises the reprobate (Psalm 15:4) but he loves the righteous. But though we hate evil we need not, should not hate the evil-doers. Nevertheless a right view of the Psalmist's attitude might put blood and iron into our piety which is in danger of seeping away and evaporating into slushy sentimentality. The Psalmist's passion for righteousness might well rouse us from our anaemic piety and moral languor and the fuller revelation that has come to us in Christ can fill us with redemptive power. So shall we be not overcome of evil but will overcome evil with good. Ours will be the Christian therapeutic.

19

THE THOUGHT OF SIN

With such a profound idea of God we may expect to find a correspondingly profound idea of Sin. Here there are many signs of growth and development. In the earlier stages of the Old Testament history, sin was conceived in objective fashion and little or no account was taken of motive. Sin was the sinful act that implied or involved damage to one's neighbor or infringed the majesty of God. It was something that could be repaired or "covered" by suitable compensation or by priestly technique. Thus in Exodus 22:15, 16 the seduction of a maid is treated as something that may be put right by a money payment: a property right had been violated. Leviticus 6:1–7 shows how a fraudulent transaction may be atoned or "unsinned" by a suitable money adjustment and ritual action. II Samuel 6:6, 7 tells of a well-intentioned countryman who thought to steady the trembling ark of God as it threatened to fall from the lumbering cart, but he was struck dead for his pains. Obviously we are here moving in the realm of tabus and superstitions, and the conception of sin has not been moralised. The conception of sin as something that damages the moral personality and injures the spirit of man was not yet known. Lying (Genesis 20:2), deception (Genesis 27:9), drunkenness (Genesis 9:21), adultery (Genesis 16:3), and suicide (I Samuel 31:4), all of which we would regard with moral horror, are recorded without any specific observation as to the sinfulness of those acts. The writers plainly did not think of these matters as we think. Ideas which had been materialised had yet to be moralised, and they were moralised by the prophets of Israel. The word *holy* did not have ethical significance before the time of Isaiah: that word simply implied *set apart* and it could be used of pots and pans reserved for the service of the sanctuary. It could even be used of the *holy women* (*qedeshoth*) set apart for ritual prostitution. Clearly there was growth and development.

The great ethical advance that came with the prophets is reflected in the Psalter. Here the singers of Israel are largely indebted to Israel's seers. This debt is obvious not so much from the extensive reference to sin as from the intense inwardness with which the subject is treated in the psalms. It is noteworthy that the number of such psalms is not large, and of the seven Penitential Psalms (6, 32, 38, 51, 102, 130, 143) two make no mention of sin (6, 102). But Psalms 32, 51, 130, reveal a depth of insight and feeling that is not surpassed elsewhere in the Old Testament. Psalm 51 may be regarded as the classic of the penitent spirit (see p. 96f.) and few things in the anthology of penitent confessions can equal it in spiritual value. Here are set forth in impressive fashion the great realities of Sin, Grace, and Forgiveness. Here sin is seen fundamentally and in its essence to be sin against God (Psalm 51:4): the sinful act is rebellion against God.

> Your iniquities have separated between you
> and your God, and your sins have hid his face
> from you, so that he will not hear.
>
> (ISAIAH 59:2)

Sin is that which severs man's fellowship with God, and without that fellowship the Hebrew could not think of life in any meaningful way.

The terms used for sin, or some of them at least, may have originally referred to the formal and objective aspect of it, but in the Psalter those terms have been filled with deep ethical and spiritual content. Just as Isaiah took the term *holy* and charged it full with new significance so that it came to signify the glorious holiness and "apartness" of God, so the Psalmist took those old terms and filled them with spiritual significance. Or rather they took those terms which had already been transmuted by the prophets and made them their own. Regard must be paid to the changing meaning of words and here the familiar Hebrew parellelism is a fairly safe guide. There are passages in the Psalter where the old formal sense may still adhere to these terms, but the choicer spirits who speak the biggest words in this matter never leave us in doubt as to their meaning.

> Full well I know my sin,
> and my transgression is ever before me.
> Against thee alone have I sinned,
> and in thy sight done evil:
> That thy word might be justified,
> and thy judgment made clear.
> In iniquity was I begotten,
> in sin did my mother conceive me.
> (PSALM 51:3–5)

The Hebrew terms are significant. The first word for sin here is *pesha‘* and it means rebellion: it centers sin in the rebellious will. The term transgression (*chattath*) means a *missing the mark,* and clearly goes back to the formal aspect of sin. But the parallelism shows clearly that the singer is not concerned with anything formal or external but with an internal corruption of the human personality that has set its will against the will of God Almighty.

We shall observe later in our consideration of the doctrine of retribution that the common belief in ancient times—and still in our own day—was that prosperity attended piety while suffering and sickness were the necessary accompaniments of sin. This belief is present in the Psalter, and may even be found in such a psalm as the fifty-first, but it is to be observed that when the psalmist complains of his suffering and pain (Psalm 51:8, 14) his prayer is not so much for relief from his pain as for the restoration of his communion with God. The restoration of that fellowship will mean the healing of all his diseases (103:5), but it will mean that only because the divine forgiveness of sin has put right the broken and distorted relation between himself and God. For to the Hebrew the world of Nature was the expression of moral purpose.

> Restore unto me the joy of thy salvation
> (PSALM 51:12).

Such is his prayer. To the Hebrew, salvation always had a large material content, but the spiritual fellowship with God was the main content without which the material availed nothing (Psalm 73:25f.).

The measure of the Psalmist's hatred and horror of sin may be gathered not only from the moving tones in which he bewails it, but from the deep peace and profound joy that fill the heart of the man whose sin is forgiven, whose transgression is covered:

> Blessed *is he whose* trangression is forgiven,
> *whose* sin is covered.

> Blessed *is* the man unto whom the Lord imputeth not iniquity, and in whose spirit *there is* no guile.
> (PSALM 32:1, 2).

Again we have sin set forth in threefold fashion as *pesha'*, *chatta*, and *'awon*, the last term signifying that which is perverted, twisted, crooked, the tortuous path of the evil-doer. The same three terms are used in Exodus 39:7 where God is revealed as "forgiving iniquity, and transgression, and sin." These same terms are used by the high priest on the Day of Atonement (*Mishna, Yoma,* 3:8). And as the terms for sin are threefold so also is it with the terms used for the forgiving grace of God. It is not only the *lifting away* of a crushing burden, as in the case of Bunyan's pilgrim, but it is the *covering over* of a stain that soils, with love that covers a multitude of sins. It is further a cancelling and *blotting out* of all our debts written in God's book. When that is done there comes to man a surpassing joy that can find expression in these opening ejaculatory words. By this act is restored the right relation between man and God. This restoration comes when man stands before God, when man is uncovered of every shame and disguise and meets his Maker in the realm of absolute truth. Every refuge of lies must be swept away and he stands on the ground of truth. And so he adds the meaningful words: "in whose spirit is no guile."

The swelling melodies of Psalms 65, 103 reveal the same deep joy and show also how the Psalmists hated the sin that separated from God. All through we sense the haunting fear that this wasting destructive thing may slip into his life:

> Who can discern his errors?
> Cleanse thou me from hidden faults.
> (PSALM 19:12)

And a man trembles as he remembers that God sets "our hidden sins in the light of his countenance" (Psalm 90:8).

When man sins, and sin has separated him from God, there is no way back to peace and joy save through penitent confession of the fault, which God meets and welcomes with the gift of forgiveness:

> I acknowledged my sin unto thee,
> and mine iniquity have I not hid.
> I said, I will confess my transgressions unto
>   the Lord;
> and thou forgavest the iniquity of my sin.
>
> (PSALM 32:5)

There is peculiar passion in the Hebrew of this verse, for the first word is *my sin* (*chattathi*) and the last word is the same. But forgiveness lifts away his sin. In so doing God vindicates his own righteousness and all ethical values are preserved and maintained (Psalm 51:4). Some of the most moving passages in all devotional literature occur in Psalms 32, 51, 130, and they move us because they are true to life as the saints in all generations confirm. Those psalms are as Pauline as Paul himself and those *Psalmi Paulini* were specially dear to the heart of Augustine. The analysis of sin here is as profound as anything found in the New Testament.

> If thou, Lord, shouldest mark iniquity,
> O Lord, who shall stand?
>
> (PSALM 130:3)

For the holy God is of purer eyes than to behold iniquity. If forgiveness is bestowed, it is with the purpose of instilling a deeper and more genuine piety in the hearts of men:

> But *there is* forgiveness with thee,
> that thou mayest be feared.
>
> (PSALM 130:4)

This is strangely emphatic in the original:

> With thee (alone) is the (only) forgiveness.

So says Barnes in his commentary on the psalm, and cites the words of Shakespere:

> Why all the souls that were, were forfeit once;
> And he that might the vantage best have took,
>   Found out the remedy.
>
> (*Measure for Measure*)

That is the never-ceasing wonder of redemption. It is an experience that awes the soul and subdues the heart of man. "Where sin abounded grace did much more abound." Over against Sin stands the divine Grace that forgives, and *forgives in a way that does full justice to moral values*. Forgiveness is not something cheap and easy: it is an act charged with moral earnestness and spiritual passion. Grace reigns and full justice is done to moral realities:

> Mercy and truth are met together;
> Righteousness and peace kiss each other.
>
> (PSALM 85:10)

Sometimes the poet will look at this from another angle and put it thus:

> Also to thee, O Lord, *belongeth* mercy (*Chesed*);
> for thou renderest to every man according to his work.
>
> (PSALM 62:12)

"The nation is the individual writ large," says Plato,[1] and whether the words be spoken of the nation or the solitary soul they alike reveal the Hebrew thought concerning sin. Perhaps the whole theology and philosophy can best be summed in one pregnant observation made by the poet of Psalm 99:

> Thou answeredst them, O Lord our God;
> thou wast a God that forgavest them,
> though thou tookest vengeance of their inventions.
>
> (PSALM 99:8)

Reference has already been made to the Pauline nature of these psalms: this can be discerned more clearly in their description of forgiveness. Here righteousness comes first and peace follows to the cleansed life. Forgiveness may not be thrown to a man as one throws a bone to a dog, nor may we speak of the divine forgiveness with the levity of Heine

[1] Plato, *Republic,* 368C.

and say, *"c'est son métier"* (it's his business). The Psalmist
does not think in such light fashion. Pearls cannot, must
not, be cast before swine. Penitence, deep and searching,
precedes forgiveness and is the ground on which God meets
man with the inestimable boon of salvation. Man may not
reverse the order here or subvert spiritual realities. There
is "no peace to the wicked."

> Righteousness marches before him,
> and Peace follows in his train.
>
> (PSALM 85:13)

"The kingdom of God," says Paul, "is righteousness and joy
and peace." These succeed each other both logically and
chronologically. Paul and the Psalmist are one on this point,
and they are one in the knowledge that peace has its price
and that forgiveness is at great cost. "By terrible things in
righteousness" we find answer from "the God of our salvation" (Psalm 65:5). For there is always the danger that
a man or nation may seek to compromise with sin and bring
about

> a peace that *is* full of wrongs and shames
> horrible, hateful, monstrous, not to be told.
>
> (Tennyson, *Maud*, Pt. 3)

The evangelical theology of the New Testament and the
saint of the old dispensation knew that righteousness must
go before peace. They seemed to sense the deep significance
of Christ's word, "Blessed are the peacemakers": they knew
that peace had to be made and that at times it might only
be made through such "terrible things" as war.

The Psalter does not deal with the origin of sin. It is
concerned only with the somber fact of its presence in
human life and with the glad fact of its removal by grace
divine. The singers know well the sovereignty of God and
the freedom of man's will, and they know that the seat and
center of sin is the human will. The later refinements of the

Rabbis with their doctrine of the good and evil impulse (*yetser hattob, yetser hara'*) are unknown to the Psalmist. Nor is there here any doctrine of Original Sin nor any thought of evil inherent in human flesh. The words of Psalm 51:5:

> In sin was I begotten,
> in iniquity did my mother conceive me,

might seem to suggest one or other or both of these ideas, but neither is really there. The poet is simply saying that sin is a racial thing, that the natural precedes the spiritual, and that man can only be "born again from above." For life itself is the gift of God, and life is not sinful.

20

THE DOCTRINE OF RETRIBUTION

The thought of Sin in the Psalter cannot be fully understood without reference to that which forms its background —the Old Testament doctrine of Retribution or Recompense.

According to the familiar word of Bacon, "Prosperity is the blessing of the Old Testament," [1] and that word summarises the matter fairly well. The Old Testament writers generally believed that prosperity is the inevitable accompaniment of piety and that, as a corollary, suffering follows upon the heels of sin. The doctrine may be interpreted at times in terms of a rank Utilitarianism, as by the Satan in Job (1:10) and in large measure by the writer of Deuteronomy, while in the historians it will yield a wholly pragmatic scheme of history. For example, we meet thirteen times in the book of Judges with some such recurring phrase as this:

> and the children of Israel did evil in the sight
> of Jehovah and forgot Jehovah their God . . .
> Therefore the anger of Jehovah was kindled
> against Israel, and he sold them into the hands
> of . . . and the children of Israel served their
> oppressors . . . years. And when the children
> of Israel cried unto Jehovah, Jehovah raised

[1] Bacon, F., *Essays: Of Adversity.*

> up a deliverer. . . . and the land had rest
> forty years.

This may be philosophy of history but it is too mechanical
to be real. The writer feels that things must have happened
that way, for he has the support of a definite theory of
divine providence. Jehovah delivers the righteous, and the
unrighteous he punishes. The righteous prosper and the
wicked suffer.

> Jehovah tests both righteous and wicked,
> And him who loves violence he doth hate.
> (PSALM 11:5, 6)

Nor is the theory as mechanical as one might think. The
belief is grounded in the Hebrew faith in the divine righteousness. The Judge of all the earth shall do right (Genesis
18:25). If there is a righteous judge above, then there can
be no moral anomalies on earth beneath. To admit the
presence of such anomalies would be to deny the righteousness of God. For to the Old Testament generally there was
no outlook beyond the bounds of time and sense. This is not
intended to deny the presence of certain gleams and glimpses
of life hereafter, but, in the main, life to the Old Testament
Hebrew did not mean more than this mortal span. Immortality was not yet brought to life. Thus things had to be put
right *here and now* and God's righteousness had to be revealed in the sphere of time. It is necessary to bear this in
mind, for frequently the theory is emphasised on its mechanical side as if it had no basis in logic or faith. The
theory came, in time, to be questioned, for life must inter-
rogate all theologies in terms of experience, and life is
larger and broader than any of its philosophies. A deeper
understanding of the divine character and of the ways of
God with man had to be thought out, and in the book of
Job we see theology locked in deadly combat with vital
experience and men attaining to a fuller view of God and
his Providence.

The doctrine, however, died hard. Perhaps old theologies never die. In the earlier period and in the simpler forms of social organisation this system of rewards and punishments may have worked fairly well. If there were exceptions to the general rule they would be such as proved the current doctrine or could be easily explained away. Abraham, Isaac, and Jacob were each rich in flocks and herds, and Job was the most prosperous and the most pious of the sons of the East. A simple commandment like, "Honor thy father and thy mother," is reinforced by the motive, "that thy days may be long in the land which the Lord thy God giveth thee" (Deuteronomy 5:16). That might not seem an adequate motive for us, but it was sufficient for the Hebrew. The goods come to the good: be good and the Lord will reward you, and the reward was construed in terms of camels and oxen (Job 1:3). But the passage of time and the increasing complexity of life disturbed the idyllic calm of Israel's simpler life, and Israel found herself among the nations and involved in all the entanglements of international politics. The Assyrian "came down like the wolf on the fold" in 701 B.C., but God delivered the righteous, and the old theology or theodicy was vindicated once more in spectacular form. But it was not always so, and soon religion was set into the interrogative mood, and we find Habakkuk, "the father of speculation in Israel," faced with a serious problem, probably in the year 516 B.C. That problem he sets forth as follows:

> Thou art of purer eyes than to behold evil, and canst look not upon iniquity, wherefore lookest thou upon them that deal very treacherously, and holdest thy peace when the wicked devoureth the man that is more righteous than he?
>
> (HABAKKUK 1:13)

The situation here is national and it was bound to emerge

first in that form. But soon we find it emerging in the case of the individual, and Jeremiah asks the same question.

> Righteous art thou, O Lord,
>> Should I dispute with thee:
> Yet concerning matters of right
>> Would I speak with thee.
> Why is the way of the wicked so smooth,
>> And all treacherous men at ease?
>
> (JEREMIAH 12:1)

The urgent interrogation, "My God, my God, why?" (Psalm 22:1), and the impatient cry "How long, O Lord, how long?" (90:13), reveal a pained sense of wonder and bewilderment in face of innocent suffering, though both seers and singers hold fast to their faith in the divine righteousness. It was reserved for Job to speak a deeper word than the Psalmist, but the profoundest word comes from the author of Isaiah 52:13–53:12.

The doctrine which thus interpreted the fact of the divine righteousness was open to serious misinterpretation. The book of Job shows all too clearly where such a doctrine might finally lead men, and how by its leading the best of friends might slay the character of their friend with a logical syllogism. For, if prosperity is the index of piety, then suffering and poverty are no less clearly the indices of sin. Thus the Old Testament can have no Gospel for the poor, for men are here deprived of God and divine consolation precisely at the point where they most need him. The corollary of the doctrine clearly is that *all sufferers are sinners.* This is the position assumed by Job's friends, and it is in this tragic light we must interpret the frequent complaint of the sick and suffering in the Psalter.

> Yea, mine own familiar friend, in whom I
>> trusted,
> Who did eat of my bread,
> Hath lifted up his heel against me.
>
> (PSALM 41:9)

We are amazed at the lack of sympathy bestowed upon the sufferer, and this fact pains the psalmists (Psalm 6:10; 40:15; 42:2). Sickness seems to bring "enemies" around a man, who leer and jeer and say, "Aha, where is now thy God?" Similar conduct, according to missionaries, is found among primitive peoples. Where sickness is interpreted as a divine visitation or due to spirits, the ordinary man is not going to interfere. Rather he will be "on the side of the angels" for his own security. It was natural and in accord with their theological inheritance that the passers-by should look on the Suffering Servant "and esteem him smitten of God and afflicted" (Isaiah 53:4). We need not blame unduly the friends of Job or be too hard on those passers-by: that was the world in which they lived and these were its beliefs and practices. For that reason we find no such thing as asceticism in the Old Testament: it may be found else-where, but it is not found here. Poverty and suffering to the Hebrew were not regarded as mere economic facts: they were regarded as judgments of God and operated as religious sanctions.

Suffering, then, is associated with sin in the Psalter. When the psalmist suffers and "all his bones do groan" he says, "I will confess my transgressions unto the Lord" (Psalm 32:5). For only two ways are open to the sufferer, the way of the psalmist or the way of Job. A man may pour out his soul in confession and find the healing grace of God (Psalms 32, 51, 103), or he may "gird up his loins," defiantly assert his innocence, and boldly challenge the righteousness of God and call in question his justice. The titanic conflict of Job does not emerge in the Psalter, though there are some close approaches to that attitude (Psalms 44, 73). The development that led to such a book as Job can be observed within the Psalter, for there we see the old doctrine being somewhat closely scanned and interrogated, and the ques-

tion of innocent suffering is frequently debated. The time
was soon to come when men would see the doctrine in conflict with experience. Men could not look on the agony and
travail of a Jeremiah without seeking to modify the old doctrine that said *all sufferers are sinners.* When men thought
of Jeremiah and his passion, they could not but say *Some
sufferers are saints,* and when later they looked on the Suffering Servant and probed the inner meaning of that sacrificial life—for the eye cannot always cheat the conscience—
they came to say, *Some sufferers are Saviors.* All that took
time and represents growth and development. At the same
time we mark the development towards a fuller thought of
life and the extension of man's interest to the other side of
things. Thoughts of immortality and resurrection were coming into men's minds. This latter growth and development
cannot be separated in the Old Testament from the doctrine
of Retribution, for Israel's hope of life hereafter is largely a
postulate drawn from experience of sorrow, national and
individual.

"All the Psalmists maintain strenuously the doctrine of
moral retribution within this life: no generalisation can be
made with greater confidence." So says H. W. Robinson.[2]
Some psalms deal with it more explicitly than others, but it
is the underlying background of the Psalter. The 37th Psalm
gives prominence to the doctrine, but a careful examination
of this psalm will show that the writer here "protesteth too
much." When a man is sure of himself he does not speak at
such length. The old doctrine is here asserted over and over
again.

> The Lord knoweth the days of the upright;
> and their inheritance shall be for ever.
> They shall not be ashamed in the evil time:
> and in the days of famine they shall be satisfied.

[2] *The Old Testament, its Making and Meaning,* p. 60.

> But the wicked shall perish,
> and the enemies of the Lord shall be as the fat of
>   lambs:
> they shall consume; into smoke shall they consume
>   away.

(VERSES 18–20)

Plainly this singer thought it best to let sleeping dogmas lie. But that may not be: someone will for ever be disturbing them. The singer may not be just "whistling to keep his courage up," but we are compelled to question his judgment when he says:

> I have been young, and *now* am old,
> yet have I not seen the righteous forsaken,
> nor his seed begging bread.   (PSALM 37:25)

There is a sense in which it is always true that the eye brings with it what it sees: it is possible for a man to wear blinkers. But a Job will not suffer himself to be blinded or fooled; he will face the facts of life and will strike out a new theology on the anvil of his own suffering heart. Old theologies, like old soldiers, never die. They just linger on and we find the thought reappearing in the New Testament:

> And his disciples asked him, saying, Master, who
> did sin, this man or his parents, that he was born
> blind?   (JOHN 9:2)

Such a belief is common enough in our own day. Psalms 49 and 73 deal with the problem more adequately and carry us forward to a more satisfying viewpoint in which life is looked at in the light of the eternal.

The "strong crying and tears" of the Psalmist and passionate prayers are to be understood in the light of this doctrinal background. Here emerge those violent anthropopathisms and those huge anthropomorphisms which are the vital soul of Old Testament religion. The vigorous language of such a psalm as 44 had its background and justification in this ancient theology.

> Wake up! why sleepest thou, O Lord?
> Awake! spurn us not for ever.
> Stand up! and be a help to us,
> And redeem us for thy mercy's sake.
>
> (VERSES 23, 26)

These men knew they were bound to God by a covenant and that *Chesed* (mercy) was between them and God. They are prepared to "storm the kingdom" and lay hold of the promises. It is not otherwise when Jeremiah prays with fulness of passion:

> Do not abhor us, for thy name's sake,
> Do not disgrace the throne of thy glory:
> Remember, break not thy covenant with us.
>
> (JEREMIAH 14:21)

It was said of Luther, "there goes the man that gets his will of God," but Luther learned that art of prayer from the psalmists. They speak so in their prayers because they believe in the divine righteousness and are certain of moral retribution.

More frequently the singer proceeds calmly on his way confident in the current theology. The righteous shall flourish like the palm trees (Psalm 92:12), or be like a tree planted by the water-courses (Psalm 1:3); not so the wicked, not so, but "like unto the chaff are they, which wind drives to and fro." Psalm 1 is usually taken as a kind of preface to the Psalter and right at the beginning we have this doctrine set forth, and enough has been said to show that this thought runs through the whole Psalter.

21

THE LIFE HEREAFTER

This thought emerges mainly in connection with the Old Testament doctrine of Retribution. The fact of innocent suffering, conjoined with the abiding belief in the divine righteousness, led men finally to a larger and fuller view. Before we look at the development here it may be well to consider the general tenor of the Psalter and of the Old Testament as a whole.

"Length of days" was what the Hebrew desired, for death offered no prospect, and death waited for all. "Whom the gods love die young" is a Greek sentiment, but to the Hebrew early death was sheer tragedy. That man should "come to his grave like a shock of corn fully ripe" (Job 5:26) seemed most fitting. For come it must to all.

> What man doth live who shall not see death?
> Shall his soul escape from the hands of Sheol?
> (PSALM 89:48)

It is precisely this thought of Sheol that makes death in the Old Testament a thing of unrelieved gloom. Sheol is the sphere that lies outside the control of Israel's God, and there men are cut off from fellowship with the divine.

> In death there is no remembrance of thee,

230

In Sheol who shall give thee thanks?

> (PSALM 6:5)

Death ends man's fellowship with God and it ends God's relations with men.

> I am cast off among the dead,
>> like the slain that lie in the grave,
> Whom thou rememberest no more;
>> and they are cut off from thy hand.

> (PSALM 88:5)

To go down to Sheol does not imply the cessation of existence, but it means being deprived of all that makes life desirable.

> In death he will take away nothing at all,
> Nor will his pomp go down after him.

> (PSALM 49:17)

Here is but the shadow of things without any real substance, life emptied of all that makes it worthy of the name of life. Sheol is the place of dusty darkness, the abode of those "who never see the light" (Psalm 49:19). There the praise of God is stilled for ever.

> The dead praise not Yah,
> Neither any that go down into silence.

> (PSALM 115:17)

Full of gloom and dark with dust is that underworld.

> Thou has brought me down into the dust of death.

> (PSALM 22:15)

This is the only reference in the Psalter to the dust of Sheol but the thought is found also in Job (Job 17:16; 21:26), upon whose spirit the dreary prospect weighs as an intolerable burden. In the Babylonian accounts we read that the food of the shades was dust, and that they drink water mingled with dust. The boundless joy the Hebrew had in beholding the light of the sun is some reflex of the hopeless prospect that faced him in death. We catch an echo of this combination of viewpoints in the closing verses of Psalm 39:

> Look away from me, that I may rejoice
> Before I go hence and be no more.

We need not concern ourselves here with the origin of this belief in Sheol, for that is largely veiled in obscurity. Suffice it here to say that it is the dominant belief in the Psalter. The question we have to ask is whether any of those singers advanced beyond this view, and whether there are definite indications of a fuller and more adequate thought. Many scholars would answer in the negative, but this attitude seems to do less than justice to the language of the psalms. It also seems to leave little room for growth and development of religious perception. Growing experience of communion with God must surely have led men to some fuller thoughts as to the nature and quality of that fellowship, and we may well expect some choice spirits to advance to a deeper understanding and enter more fully into "the secret of the Lord." Oesterley holds that Persian influence operated in this development, and while this may not be denied it is possible to set too great store on alien influences and too little on the native spiritual vitality of Israel's religion. The Hebrew faith had sufficient dynamic in itself to force its way to this fuller prospect. The particular sphere in which that spiritual vitality operates was precisely that with which we have been dealing, the problem of innocent suffering. That is clearly the case in Job 19:25ff. and in Psalms 16, 17, 49, 73.

We need not deal here with the passage in Job: the reference to the hereafter in that passage is disputed by many scholars but there seems no real reason to deny its presence. The presence of such a belief in the Psalter is contested by many scholars, but it is difficult to resist the force of the cumulative evidence. It will at least reward us to examine that evidence. The first of these so-called *Immortality Psalms* (Psalm 16) differs from the others inasmuch as the circumstances of the singer do not seem to be distressful. This man has walked closely with God and material prosperity has followed as the divine seal of approval upon his piety. God has been gracious to him, and the communion with God has been so real and continuous that the writer is unable to think of its being interrupted or broken by death. There is a quality in that fellowship with God which must endure. And so he reaches the conclusion:

> Therefore my heart rejoices and my soul exults,
> And my body surely dwells in security;
>
> For thou wilt not abandon me to Sheol,
> Nor permit thy loved one to see the Pit.
>
> Thou wilt show me the path of life:
> Fulness of joy is in thy presence,
> And pleasures in thy right hand for evermore.
>
> (PSALM 16:10, 11)

What the writer feels here is that he has been gripped with a love that will not let him go: this love is stronger than death and will not suffer death to carry off the victory. We note that here, for it is on this assurance that whatever we find of immortality in the Old Testament ultimately rests: *it rests on an empirical fact.*

Psalm 17 springs from a different background. Here the singer is facing the fact that the wicked prosper and the righteous suffer. But the singer will not surrender his faith in the divine righteousness. He is absolutely confident of "an ultimate decency of things," and he might have said with R. L. Stevenson, "aye, and though I woke in hell I would still believe in it." [1] And thus he thinks a long, long thought, and opens the endless prospect.

> As for me, in righteousness will I behold thy face;
> I shall be satisfied when I awake with thy appearance.
>
> (PSALM 17:15)

[1] *Letters of R. L. Stevenson,* Vol. IV, p. 246 (Biographical Edition).

Here the poet is centering on the divine righteousness and making the bold leap of faith. All he has seen of God teaches him to trust God for what he cannot see. There is no need to evacuate the words of their significance or refer them to anything less than the thought of abiding communion with God.

Psalm 49 deals immediately with the problem of suffering. Here the poet is face to face with the question of the divine righteousness and here we must follow the development of thought. The poet here is very practical and he knows, as the poet of Psalms 37 and 73 knew, that there is no more consuming passion than envy. Men are robbed of their equanimity through envy of the prosperous, but it is not so with the poet and it need not be so with others. It all depends on the viewpoint one takes, and he offers a new and surprising viewpoint. For he looks at wealth and prosperity from the viewpoint of death and God. The riches of the ungodly need not rob the godly of their peace of mind or steal from them their equanimity. Fear and envy may be eradicated and inward peace may be restored. The poet tells how this may come to pass: he has looked at those things in a new and satisfying light. For we fear and envy the rich because we evaluate their wealth from the viewpoint of life. *But what if we evaluate their wealth from the viewpoint of death?* That is the revelation and insight which visited the mind of the poet. His eyes are opened and he views those things that seemed so bright and shining against the background of death. That gives a man a totally different view and leads to another estimate.

For death sets a limit to all man's efforts. Men may fume and fret at its "Thus far and no farther," but the limit is fixed and immovable. Here man finds himself faced with a might that is beyond his power to overcome. All his costliest efforts and grandiose purposes break upon it. Here is something that finally defeats and frustrates. For human power and divine power differ not quantitatively but qualitatively. Man may rage and storm against God in his desire to live for ever but it may not be. "The Everlasting Nay" is spoken, and "a gravestone is laid upon our purpose." Life is shown finally to be "but a vapor." There is nothing here to envy. This is not the pessimism of Ecclesiastes: it is the realism of insight. The poet sees things as they really are, he sees them in the light of the eternal.

> The grave is their eternal home,
> the place of their everlasting dwelling,
> though once they gave their names to lands.
> Such is the way of those who have self-confidence,
> and the latter-end of those who boast with their
> mouths.
> Like sheep they go down to Sheol
> with Death to shepherd them:
> Straight down to the grave they go,
> and their form wastes away in their home below.

These verses (11, 13, 14) are somewhat difficult to translate, but the foregoing seems to be the meaning of the original. In verse 15 the writer sets forth the other side of things and his insight here has seemed so startling to many scholars that they attempt to remove it or explain it away. Here we have one of those strange gleams that shine for a brief moment and then are gone: the thought of the poet is too vast for him to comprehend. It does not tarry but it leaves a radiant certainty, as it does also in the case of Job (19:23f.) or Jeremiah (31:31f.) or the poet of Psalm 73 (73:23f.). All those great insights of the Old Testament are fractured and broken and the great seminal thought must await a later generation for its full interpretation. The divine righteousness is vindicated in the end of the wicked, and it is vindicated again in the reward of the godly:

> But God will ransom my soul
> from the hand of Sheol:
> For he will take me.   (PSALM 49:15)

Over against Death the poet sees a power greater than Death, the God who has set Death as the end of life. As to how he will be ransomed he does not say: whether he will be translated like Elijah and Enoch or whether he will share in a resurrection with the righteous, he does not say. He is concerned only with the certainty of the fact, not with the method of its achievement. The righteous God will do righteousness, and the poet is satisfied with a satisfaction that nothing can destroy.

In the light of this revelation the singer can proceed with his task. His concern is to fortify men for the strife of life and enable them to conquer. We may translate what follows in this way:

> So have no fear if one grows rich,
> and the pomp of his house increases.
> In death he will take away nothing at all,
> nor will his pomp go down after him.
> Though he deemed himself blessed in his lifetime,
> and men praised him for faring so well,
> Yet shall he come to the race of his fathers
> who see the light no more for ever.
>
> (PSALM 49:16–19)

"Verily they have their reward" (Matthew 6:2, 5, 16): the Greek in this word of our Lord is very expressive. It means, "they have it out and out, they have received all they are to get." They have nothing more to look forward to. But it shall be well with the righteous. They have a sure hope and earnest expectation. This may not contain the full thought of resurrection or after-life but we have here a step in that direction. God will not forsake the righteous nor abandon those who hope in him.

But it is in the 73rd Psalm that we find the fullest development. This psalm represents a peak point in Old Testament piety. Here the singer sounds depths and scales heights that are beyond the reach of lesser men. It sets forth the spiritual pilgrimage of a soul that had to struggle against overwhelming doubt and win at last an assured faith at great expense of spirit. Like Dostoievsky he might say,

> My Hosanna has burst forth from a huge furnace
> of doubt.[2]

This is the most significant of all the Wisdom Psalms. It might be called an epitome of the book of Job but it is more significant than the book of Job in that the stake here is higher. The question here is the question of faith's validity and it is discussed with a weight of passion and wealth of insight that are unmatched by anything else in the Old Testament. It ascends heights that not even Job could climb and it opens endless prospects. It looks out on "the land of far distances" and links itself closely with the New Testament revelation.

The date of the psalm would seem to be between Job and Ecclesiastes: it differs from the older Wisdom literature in that it is less objective and reveals a strong personal element. There is here a trembling passion that bespeaks something of the agony and bloody sweat which have attended the soul's pilgrimage. Kittel uses for title of this song "Das grosse Dennoch" (*The great Nevertheless*) and this represents well the deep emotion and glad release that are inherent in the song. It is as if when a man has struggled with a sea of troubles and, exhausted and sore-spent, finds his footing once more and with a sense of emancipation breathes the word, "At last."

It is worth while tracing this man's progress to a triumphant faith. The poet is frank in the analysis of his own life and thought. It was envy, deadliest of all the deadly sins, that moved him to this train of thought. His view centered on externals (*verses* 2–5). He was envious of those who were fat and sleek and wallowed in the abundance of this world's

---

[2] *Dostoievsky: an Interpretation*, by N. Berdyaev, p. 31.

goods. Why should it be so well with those who compro-
mised the faith of the fathers and why should it be so ill
with those who regulated their lives by God's holy law?
Such conditions made faith difficult. The poet waxes hot as
he thinks of the cruelty and oppression the rich practiced on
the poor and humble. Proud and high-handed they strut
about and mouth lofty words against high heaven. It may
be they posed as representatives of the new order, belonging
to the "Age of Enlightenment," and, inasmuch as most folk
would rather be out of the world than out of fashion, they
did not lack a considerable following. Verse 10 is difficult to
translate but we would read it thus:

> Small wonder that people resort to them,
> and drink deep draughts of their lore.

There was at this period a deep moral corruption spreading
through the body politic from the top downwards. There
was a lack of reverence towards God, and it may be that,
with the entrance of new-fangled ways, a process of rationalisation with reference to deity was in vogue (verse 11).
Men were speaking at this time of "world reason" and were
glib in their discussion of "cosmic principles." The old idea
of God who hears and answers prayer was outmoded: God
seemed to have receded into the distant spaces. In Ecclesiastes he seems little more than a faint memory and as unde-
fined as "Fate." And so with their blasphemies they said,
"How doth God know, and is there knowledge with the most
High?" The God-idea had no reality for them. But no one is
likely to feel awe in the presence of a cosmic principle or
worry about his responsibility to "world reason."

This affects the poet's faith in God. Hitherto he has centered on externals; now he becomes analytical and intro-
spective. The combined pressure from without and within is
almost too much for faith: his inner life is well-nigh ship-
wrecked. So dark do things appear that he is almost pre-

pared to give up religion altogether (verses 13, 14). That would be to accept the universe on its own terms and would be nothing more than sullen dumb resignation. But the poet was withheld from this final treachery and from that last base denial:

> If I say I will speak thus:
> Behold I should offend against the generation of
> thy children.

Religion may have brought him nothing tangible, but it had left him with the feeling that he must keep the peace with his own conscience and be able to interview his own heart without shame. It is the thought of loyalty to the community that arrests him and brings him to a stop before the final disaster. Was he minister to a group of *the Saints?* He will not "cause one of these little ones to offend." That would be treason in the highest and something precious within his own soul would surely die.

This thought of responsibility to others does not solve the problem. Life is still a riddle: he must press on in his quest. No explanation is possible on the human level. It is only when the poet perceives the bankruptcy of human thought and seeks elsewhere that he finds. Man's extremity becomes the divine opportunity, and only a divine revelation will suffice. Here comes the "Copernican change" and the center is shifted from earth to heaven, from time to eternity (*verse* 17). The word "sanctuary" is in the plural form and something more than what we mean by sanctuary is intended. It corresponds in some degree to the Pauline phrase "in the heavenlies" (*en tois ouranois*); it suggests something mystical, that the poet has been admitted to "the secret of the Lord." He stands within Jehovah's council. Like Isaiah in the temple vision (Isaiah 6), the poet now sees things as he never saw them before. He has come to a place that is full of light. Now he sees the ungodly in the light of their end (literally, *afterness*), and we need not be concerned to put limitations on the idea suggested by the word "end." Verses 19, 20 may be rendered thus:

> How suddenly are they brought to nought,
> and come to a final end in terror!
>
> Vanished as a dream on wakening,
> Whose image the waker despises.

It may be that the poet is saying no more than the old theology had said, and again it may be that he is saying more. For it must often have come to pass in the Persian and Greek period that men were suddenly thrown out of office and even brought to ignominious death. There was enough of that to make wise men feel that though

> the mills of God grind slowly
> Yet they grind exceeding small.
>> (F. VON LOGAU, "Retribution")

If that were all the poet had to say we might still be standing with the old theology of recompense and in the company of Job's friends. This, however, is the beginning of his insight. The abiding realities come to view and in their light he proceeds to reorientate his whole life and thought. For God's thoughts are not man's thoughts, and this man now shares the thought of God. He stands in the divine secret. The things that vexed have passed away. Like insubstantial figures in a dream they harass no more. Now there is only the overwhelming reality of God: all his past fuming and fretting seem stupid (*verses* 21, 22). Now, like Job, he confesses his folly and bows himself in humility before God to rise with this shout of triumph:

> Nevertheless—I *am* continually with thee;
> thou hast holden *me* by my right hand.
>
> Thou shalt guide me with thy counsel,
> and afterward receive me to glory.
>
> Whom have I in heaven *but thee?*
> and *there is* none upon earth *that* I desire beside thee.

My flesh and my heart faileth:
but God *is* the strength of my heart,
and my portion for ever.   (VERSES 23–26)

There is nothing to equal this in the Old Testament. Here the poet soars into the empyrean and beholds the radiant certainty in abiding communion.

It may be permitted here to look back on the way by which this poet traveled in his pilgrimage from darkness to light. In the retrospect we come to understand what he meant by the word "their latter end" in verse 17, and also the precise significance of the word, "afterward thou takest me to glory" (*verse* 24). The one insight produced the other. In the light of "the afterness" all earthly things, prosperity and poverty alike, assume a new aspect and are properly assessed. All such things are seen now in the light of the eternal; the veil is torn away. The limitations of time and space are transcended. The poet here has passed beyond the writer of the 37th Psalm and the book of Job—he may be indebted to the poet of the 49th Psalm—and he is the first to burst into a new and larger sphere: he concerns himself with values that are spiritual, God, heaven, glory. Something outside the physical realm is plainly intended here, and for that reason the material aspect of things is of no further moment, whether these material things pertain to the godly or the ungodly.

This can only mean for the poet that death is not the end but that there is something beyond, an "afterness." The words *achar* (*afterward*), *laqach* (*take*), and *kabod* (*glory*) have each eschatological significance. *Laqach* is almost a technical term for translation and is used of Enoch (Genesis 5:24) and Elijah (II Kings 2:9), as also of the Suffering Servant in Isaiah 53:8. The poet does not tell how this will be accomplished for him, whether by translation or resurrection, but he is sure of the fact that he will not finally be separated from God. Communion with the everlasting God will not be broken by death: there is an "afterward" beyond death. In the light of that fact all earthly ills are forgotten: we can, in the words of the Apostle, "rejoice in our present sufferings," conscious of the glory that shall be revealed, which even now we may enjoy in foretaste. The prosperity of the godless may go with them to the grave but it goes no further. It may be stripped from them while they are yet alive, but their reward is not exhausted in the desolations of time. Here we have an advance beyond Psalm 49: there is an "afterward" and a moral continuity beyond death. They will receive their recompense, as will also the righteous, for the one will be near and the other far from God (verses 27, 28). "He who has God," says Weiser, "has life: without God there is death." To be near to God is to have a good beyond compare, to have life for evermore.

It may not be right to read into those words more than they contain but we must not take out of them less than they really express. The full Christian doctrine of immortality may not be here but there is here the thought and assurance of something that lies behind every doctrine of the after-life. It is the thought that God is stronger than death, the assurance that, when a man has formed a friendship with God, he has forged a bond which death cannot break. The same thought is expressed in the words of Jesus:

> Now, that the dead are raised, even Moses showed at the bush, when he calleth the Lord the God of Abraham, and the God of Isaac, and the God of Jacob.
>
> For he is not a God of the dead, but of the living: for all live unto him.   (LUKE 20:37, 38)

By that Jesus meant to say that the Syrian stars were not looking down on the graves of the patriarchs, but that the patriarchs were looking down on the Syrian stars. They were not "has-beens" swept away in the stream of time. They had

formed a friendship with God and had been gripped by his
love, and that love held them up and carried them through
the last cold river of death.

> Many waters cannot quench love, neither can the
> floods drown it; if a man would give all the sub-
> stance of his house for love, it would utterly be
> contemned.   (SONG OF SONGS, 8:7)

Those patriarchs now serve God day and night in his temple.
That is what Jesus says, and it is what the Psalmist said.
Thus in similar terms the Apostles interpreted the Resurrec-
tion of Jesus:

> It was not possible that he should be holden of
> death.   (ACTS 2:24)

Otherwise the victory would not be to love and faith. And
so Paul also writes:

> Death hath no dominion over him.
>   (ROMANS 6:9)

For Paul felt that such faith as Jesus had revealed had in
itself the guarantee of immortality. It seemed impossible
to conceive that such a life of intimate communion with the
Father could be broken or interrupted by an alien force like
death. As men looked on that life of absolute faith which
the Son lived, in full abandon and complete surrender to the
Father's will, so that it was the Son's meat and drink to do
that will, they felt certain that such intimacy and communion could not be rent and broken but must grow from more
to more. They knew love was mightier than death, that
"none can pluck them from my Father's hand." The New
Testament is here setting up the omnipotent divine love and
human faith as the twin pillars on which an adequate doctrine of future life must finally rest. They spoke the words
we have cited not only by reason of their knowledge of God's
love but also by reason of what they had seen of faith in the
life of Jesus. Such faith could not be disappointed. God

would be unworthy—let us say it in all reverence—to be called the God of trusting men if he failed to answer such faith and vindicate it. The New Testament implies as much when it says:

> Wherefore He is not ashamed to be called their
> God.   (HEBREWS 11:16)

The Judge of all the earth does righteousness. We need not be ashamed of God, and again we may say reverently God does not need to be ashamed of himself.

Thus we reach a doctrine of future life that rests not on a metaphysical but on an empirical basis, being built ultimately on the essential character of God as love and the nature of faith itself. Here is the attitude of a little child that puts its hand in the hand of its father and is content to trust him in all circumstances, for the child knows that the father's love will triumph over every barrier and lead it to the ultimate goal. To mention death in the presence of such faith and love is an irrelevance and impertinence. Love is stronger than death and mightier far. God despoils the strong man armed. Thus we can have eternal life in the midst of time. Nothing matters beside that. We may lack health, wealth, and prosperity, which once the Psalmist envied, but we have God for our portion for ever.

"If God is for us who can be against us?" (Romans 8:31). "These are great thoughts," says Kittel, "in presence of which we stand amazed." It is the greatest thing the human heart has come to know, and it is not surpassed, though it is equalled, by Saint Paul in his reference to Christ:

> Who shall separate us from the love of Christ? Shall tribulation, or distress, or persecution, or famine, or nakedness, or peril, or sword?
> For I am persuaded that neither death, nor life, nor angels, nor principalities, nor powers, nor things present, nor things to come,

Nor height, nor depth, nor any other creature, shall be able to separate us from the love of God, which is in Christ Jesus our Lord.

(ROMANS 8: 35, 38, 39)

That only makes explicit what was implicit in the great "Nevertheless" of the Psalmist.

SELECTED BIBLIOGRAPHY

A. *General Introductions to the Old Testament* by S. R. Driver, W. O. E. Oesterley and T. H. Robinson, R. H. Pfeiffer, H. W. Robinson, Otto Eissfeldt, Ernst Sellin.
Bewer, Julius A., *The Literature of the Old Testament in its Historical Development* (revised edition, New York, 1944)
Gunkel, Herrmann, *Einleitung in die Psalmen,* completed by J. Begrich (1933)

B. *Old Testament Theology*
Eichrodt, Walther, *Theologie des Alten Testaments,* (3 vols., Leipzig, 1933–39)
Köhler, Ludwig, *Theologie des Alten Testaments,* (Tübingen, 1936)
Sellin, Ernst, *Theologie des Alten Testaments,* (Leipzig, 1933)

C. *Commentaries on the Psalms*
Barnes, W. E., *The Psalms,* (Westminster Commentaries, 2 vols., London, 1931)
Buttenweiser, M., *The Psalms,* (Chicago, 1938)
Cheyne, T. K., *The Book of Psalms,* (New York, 1888)
Duhm, Bernhard, *Die Psalmen,* (2nd edition, Tübingen, 1922)

248 *Selected Bibliography*

Freehof, Solomon B., *The Book of Psalms*, (Cincinnati, 1938)

Gunkel, Herrmann, *Die Psalmen*, (Göttinger Handkommentar, 4th edition, 1926)

Herkenne, Heinrich, *Das Buch der Psalmen*, (Bonn, 1936)

Kittel, Rudolf, *Die Psalmen*, (Kommentar zum A. T., Leipzig, 5–6th edition, 1929)

Oesterley, W. O. E., *The Psalms*, (2 vols., London, 1939)

Schmidt, Hans, *Die Psalmen*, (Handbuch zum A. T., Tübingen, 1934)

Staerk, W., *Die Schriften Des A. T., Abteilung III, Band 1* (Göttingen, 1920)

D. *General Works* (dealing with literary, critical, religious, and theological questions)

Budde, Karl, *Die Schönsten Psalmen*, (Leipzig, 1915)

Davison, W. T., *The Praises of Israel*, (London, 1902)

Dinsmore, C. A., *The English Bible as Literature*, (Boston, 1931)

Gordon, A. R., *The Poets of the Old Testament*, (London, 1912)

Gunkel, Herrmann, *Ausgewählte Psalmen*, (4th edition, Göttingen, 1917)

Gunkel, Herrmann, *What Remains of the Old Testament*, translated by A. K. Dallas, (London, 1927)

James, Fleming, *Thirty Psalmists*, (New York, 1938)

Löhr, M., *Psalmenstudien*, (BWAT, NF, Heft 3: Berlin, 1922)

MacDonald, D. B., *The Hebrew Literary Genius*, (Princeton, 1933)

McFadyen, J. E., *The Psalms in Modern Speech*, (3rd edition, London, no date)

Mowinckel, Sigmund, *Psalmenstudien I. Awen und die*

individuellen Klagepsalmen, (1921); *II. Das Thronbesteigungsfest und der Ursprung der Eschatologie* (1922); *III. Kultprophetie und prophetische Psalmen* (1923); *IV. Die technischen Termini in den Psalmenüberschriften* (1923); *V. Segen und Fluch in Israel's Psalmendichtung* (1924); *VI. Die Psalmendichter* (1924)

Oesterley, W. O. E., *A Fresh Approach to the Psalter*, (London, 1937)

Patton, John H., *Canaanite Parallels in the Book of Psalms*, (Baltimore, 1944)

Pedersen, Johannes, *Israel, its Life and Culture, I–II*, (London, 1926)

Quell, G., *Das Kultische Problem der Psalmen*, (BWAT, NF, Heft 11, Berlin, 1926)

Simpson, D. C., (ed.) *Old Testament Essays*, (Society for Old Testament Study, London, 1927)

Simpson, D. C., *The Psalmists*, (London, 1926)

Smith, J. M. P., *The Psalms*, (Chicago, 1926)

Snaith, N. H., *The Jewish New Year Festival*, (London, 1947)

Vischer, Wilhelm, *Psalmen*, (Basel, 1944)

Volz, Paul, *Das Neujahrfest Jahwes*, (Laubhüttenfest, Tübingen, 1912)

Weiser, Artur, *Die Psalmen ausgewählt, übersetzt, und erklärt*, (Göttingen, 1935, 2nd edition, 1939)

Welch, Adam C., *The Psalter, in Life, Worship, and History*, (London, 1926)

Willoughby, H. R., *The Study of the Bible Today and Tomorrow*, (Chicago, 1947)

Zimmern, H., *Babylonische Hymnen und Gebete*, (2nd edition, Leipzig, 1911)

INDEX OF SCRIPTURE TEXTS

OLD TESTAMENT

251

INDEX OF NAMES AND SUBJECTS